Inverness
and the
Great Glen

compiled by
Christopher J. Uncles

Fort Augustus from Loch Ness.

Archd. Macintyre, Fort William

Caledonian Canal.

The deck of an Inverness-bound steamer provides the photographer with a panorama of Fort Augustus about 1900 showing the Benedictine monastery, the pepper-box lighthouse beside the Caledonian Canal and Inveroich Pier (on the right). The monastery stands on the site of the former fort whose grounds extended across to Inveroich before Thomas Telford's canal was cut. There, just out of sight, the fort's bakery and brewery were located, together with the Barrack-master's house, known today as Inveroich House.

Stenlake Publishing Ltd
2011

FOREWORD

In seeking out collectable material over many years, I must have examined hundreds of thousands of items – postcards, photographs, glass slides and ephemera. That leads me to an aspect of collecting that I had fully intended to highlight in an earlier book, and that is the desirability of having sufficient detail on such items to aid proper identification. I call it the "who, what, where and when" of photographs. All too often one comes across tantalising images of Victorian and Edwardian ladies and gentlemen dressed in their Sunday best for the photographer, people at work or play, miscellaneous views or buildings, soldiers in military uniform or events of one kind or another. Sadly they all have a common denominator: no one thought it necessary to add a name, a location or a date on the reverse of the image which, as a result, may remain forever anonymous – a ghost of the past. Perhaps, this little reminder will encourage readers to re-appraise those photographs carefully stored at the back of a cupboard, and add to them some of the "who, what, where and when" for the benefit of their families and successive generations.

Christopher J. Uncles

Cutting for new road, Loch Ness, July 1932.

ACKNOWLEDGEMENTS

I should like to acknowledge the generous assistance given by: The Editor and Ann Johnston of *The Inverness Courier* for newspaper reports of the 1903 Beauly traction engine accident; to Lesley Junor (of Highland Council's Photographic Archive) for permission to reproduce two images from my collection which are within the Council's copyright of the David Whyte Collection; to the West Highland Museum of Fort William for a photograph of the Banavie Hotel; finally to Angela, my wife, for all her practical support and encouragement.

© 2011 Christopher J. Uncles
First Published in the United Kingdom, 2011
Stenlake Publishing Limited
54-58 Mill Square, Catrine, KA5 6RD
01290 551122
www.stenlake.co.uk

ISBN 9781840335477

Printed by
Creative Colour Bureau
1 Queen Elizabeth Avenue
Hillington Park, Glasgow
G52 4NQ
0141 891 4700
www.ccb.co.uk

The author and publishers regret that they cannot supply copies of any pictures featured in this book under any circumstances.

"If I were asked to indicate the most romantic inland voyage in Europe I would vote for the journey up or down the Caledonian Canal. The Rhine cannot hold a candle to it."

In Search of Scotland, H.V. Morton, 1929

INTRODUCTION

The major geological depression which effectively slashes the Highlands diagonally in two, from the gentle shores of the Moray Firth to Loch Linnhe and the mountainous west, is known by a variety of names – the Great Glen of Albyn, Gleann Mòr or more commonly, simply as The Great Glen. Geologists tell us that some 400 million years ago this feature was created by gigantic forces emanating from within the earth's interior which caused the earth's crust to tear, fold and fault. The subsequent eroding action of wind and wave, and later by retreating glaciers deepened, moulded and softened the Great Glen fault, the combined consequences of which resulted in a natural valley 60 miles in length which was ideally suited to east/west trade from earliest times.

Much later, in the 18th and 19th centuries, two men from widely differing backgrounds brought their ingenuity and outstanding skills to improve accessibility and ease movement around and through the Great Glen. They were General George Wade, Commander in Chief of King George I's forces in North Britain, and that "engineer extraordinary" Thomas Telford. The General's network of roads and bridges was primarily designed to assist the military penetrate areas previously the preserve of the rebellious clans, while the motivation for Thomas Telford's Caledonian Canal was commercial – and in particular to avoid heavy shipping losses in the tempestuous seas often encountered along the north coast. He cleverly adapted this landscape gifted by Nature to link the lochs in the Great Glen left behind by the last Ice Age with his Caledonian Canal. By such means he completed a cross-country waterway for small sea-going vessels, especially fishing boats, which could avoid the hazardous circuit around the Pentland Firth and Cape Wrath. However, for various reasons the canal never achieved the expectations of its protagonists. Today the accent is very much on pleasure cruisers and hire boats, and while the area is well served by roads, the most pleasant way to properly appreciate the scenic gems the Great Glen has to offer is by a leisurely progress along the waterway itself.

Inverness, at the northern end of the Glen, has had a long and eventful history. The 'Highland Capital' now has city status and owes its original founding to geographical factors as routes long used by travellers and trade converge here. Nearby at Culloden Moor, on 16th April, 1746 a bloody battle – the last fought on British soil – resulted in the Duke of Cumberland's Hanoverian army crushing, once and for all, Jacobite aspirations for a Stuart Restoration. Despite a ransom of £30,000 on his head, Prince Charles Edward Stuart was never betrayed and he escaped abroad into exile. The savage reprisals and repression which followed Culloden were reinforced by the Disarming Act of 1746. Weapons were confiscated, the Gaelic language was proscribed as was the wearing of the plaid, apart from those who were serving in the royal army. The clan system which had existed for centuries was virtually destroyed as a dark period settled over the Highlands.

A number of 'Big Houses' are featured, some of which have vanished, while the dispersal of the historic contents of Culloden House in 1897 is documented. Employing often large numbers of domestic and estate staff such houses tended to flourish before 1914, but the horrific loss of life in the Great War and the economic depression which followed, brought a tide of changed circumstances and an inexorable decline in the fortunes of many estates. Those "in service" worked long hours, their whole world revolving around the happenings in the "Big House" and the ever-changing seasonal demands of the estate.

This book is complementary to *Lochaber and the Road to the Isles* which covers the Fort William area, Ardnamurchan and Mallaig. As before, I have sought to bring together a variety of images from days long gone to give a flavour of a vanished way of life. There are four picture sequences around the Great Glen: Beauly and Glen Urquhart; Inverness; Culloden and Loch Ness (East) and Glen Moriston (via Fort Augustus) to Loch Linnhe.

BEAULY AND GLEN URQUHART

This section takes an anti-clockwise route from Inverness, taking in Beauly, Strath Glass and Glen Urquhart, returning to Muirtown on the Caledonian Canal.

These days Inverness experiences a fairly constant heavy volume of road traffic which at peak times approaches grid-lock, perhaps a reflection of its elevation to city status in recent years. And this despite the completion of two absolutely key infrastructure improvements undertaken since 1976. The first was the building of the Kessock Bridge (1976-82) which made the historic ferry to the Black Isle redundant and which now carries the re-routed A9 over the Moray Firth and onwards to the Far North. I recall that a hitch in the final stages resulted in the central span remaining uncompleted for six weeks while a strike was resolved. Simultaneously a link was provided with the Longman and Harbour Industrial Estates, a link that was further strengthened by the second development. Friars Bridge (1984-6) was built as an entirely new crossing of the River Ness, greatly enhancing cross-river traffic and giving connections with the A862 for Clachnaharry and Beauly, and the A82 for Fort William and the west.

By way of contrast, a glance at a late Victorian map of Inverness emphasises just how much the town has expanded in the intervening years. Then, apart from two pedestrian footbridges, there were just two road bridges across the river: the Waterloo Bridge (built 1816) giving access to the harbour quays and the Kessock Ferry, and the town's "traffic suspension bridge" (built 1850-5) used by through traffic. At that time the population of Inverness was largely concentrated on the eastern side of the river, and on the opposite side where relatively few roads had been built there was much open ground, fields and nurseries up to Muirtown on the Caledonian Canal. Here there were two roads of particular importance: Fairfield Road, of which more at the end of this section, and Telford Street by which a crossing of the canal was made at Muirtown Bridge to reach Clachnaharry.

In the early part of the twentieth century this small village on the Great North Road to Beauly was a thriving, independent community complete with its own identity, "local characters", and a history of clan rivalry which came to a head in 1378 in the Battle of Clachnaharry, marked today by a monument. Nowadays, the complete infilling of the once rural landscape up to and beyond the Caledonian Canal has resulted in a continuously built-up area so that the former village has now become to all intents and purposes an integral part of Inverness by which it has been absorbed.

Clachnaharry. J. Mackay, Inverness.

Clachnaharry Station, c.1903. The railway station on the Highland Railway opened in 1869, but closed in May 1913. The Great North Road takes a sharp double bend here over a bridge and the iron road to reveal extensive views to the Black Isle and along the wooded fringes of the firth towards Beauly, twelve miles distant.

DELMORE ROAD HOUSE BEAULY ROAD INVERNESS

A.4082. DELMORE ROAD HOUSE, BEAULY ROAD, INVERNESS, (INTERIOR)

A rare example of Art Deco architecture in the Highlands, the Delmore Roadhouse once provided food for travellers and fuel for their vehicles. The interior image of 1936 is evocative of days long gone: sturdy, old-fashioned coat and hat stands, neatly laid tables with china, three-tiered cake stands and menus – everything ready to refresh those travelling the Great North Road. But, sadly times change and no such experience has been available for many years. Later adapted as a car showroom, the site is currently used for motorcycle sales.

Shortly after leaving Delmore, the baronial turrets of Bunchrew House (now an hotel) can be seen among trees down by the shores of the Beauly Firth. Part of the house dates to the seventeenth century, and here President Forbes (of whom more later) was born. The Bunchrew Burn formed the time-honoured boundary between the Bunchrew and Lovat (Fraser) Estates. All along this coast between Inverness and Beauly, the hinterland is both well-wooded and hilly. Even today there remains something of a feeling of secretiveness about the inland straths and remoter glens, and it is unsurprising that up to the end of Queen Victoria's reign, illicit whisky distillation and smuggling were rife in such a landscape which local excisemen must have found difficult to police.

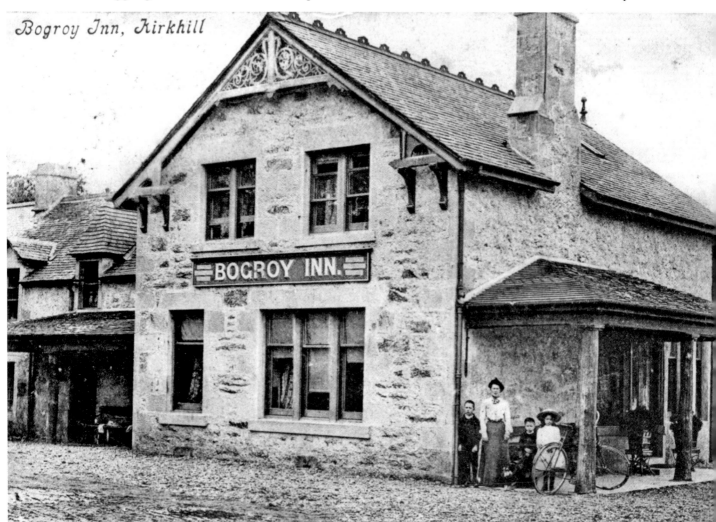

Bogroy Inn, Kirkhill

Nor is it surprising that the Bogroy Inn, pictured here *c.*1900, should have been drawn into such activities. The inn stands where a 'B' classification road joins the main highway to provide an alternative way to Beauly, via Kirkhill village. Situated just a mile inland from the firth, the inn became a natural focus for some well-documented tales of "cat and mouse" encounters with excisemen during the nineteenth century. Since 2005 the old, familiar name has been dropped, and the inn is now known as the Old North Inn.

A *cul de sac* in Kirkhill gives access to Wardlaw Cemetery which is set on rising ground and approached through an old arched gateway. "Wardlaw" is understood to be derived from ward-law or watch hill, which in this case overlooks the rich farmland bordering the Beauly Firth. The centrepiece of the cemetery is the Lovat Mausoleum built by the mason William Ross in 1633-4, and Lovat chiefs were buried here until 1815 since when interments have taken place in the family burial ground at Eskadale on the Beaufort Estate. The present indifferent state of the mausoleum externally and internally is hardly commensurate with its great historical significance which resonates with clan members worldwide. If entry is required, contact must be made with the custodian of the key who resides nearby.

In a small area of the cemetery I noted several memorials to members of the Cameron family. Originating from Clunes in Lochaber they acquired the 265-acre Fingask Estate in Kirkhill and renamed it "Clunes" in memory of their former home...

Adjoining West Lodge in Kirkhill are two old gate pillars, once part of the former carriage driveway to Clunes House which lay about 600 yards down on the flat lands of the Beauly Firth amidst farmland and its own policies, known originally as the Fingask Estate. The house, seen here about 1905, is thought to have been built in the 1850s-60s and was subsequently enlarged to accommodate family members returning from the Colonies who temporarily resided at Achnagairn House locally. Clunes House remained in Cameron ownership until about 1953 when a disastrous fire occurred while extensive dry rot was being eradicated. Demolition followed shortly thereafter, and stone from the ruins was used to build other properties close by. Contents salved went to Fraser's Auction Rooms in Inverness, from which a local resident told me she had acquired a slightly fire-damaged carpet. In 1960 the railway closed Clunes platform which had served the estate.

Achnagairn House, 1922. The house, as seen today, was built in the early years of the nineteenth century, but the fact that a date-stone of 1663 was incorporated into the library fireplace may suggest that the present house was not the first on this site. Achnagairn means "Field of the Cairns", and over time the house has developed, retaining internal and external features such as the attractive bell-shaped towers. Used as a hospital during the Second World War, subsequent years of neglect might well have proved terminal. Over recent years the present owners have implemented a substantial programme of restoration and the venue now caters for weddings and corporate events.

On the south side of the road to Beauly there are two noteable estates hidden in the landscape; the first of these is Belladrum. The entrance lodge dates from 1860, while a mile further on lies the substantial walled garden, a row of estate workers' cottages (1914) and, built on a truly heroic scale, the steading (c.1805) to which a tower was added fifty years later. In the parish of Kiltarlity *New Statistical Account* of 1845, the Rev C. Fraser gives the estate acreage as 4,300 acres composed of arable (700), pasture (2,600) and woodland (1,000). Down by the Belladrum Burn, which joins the River Beauly, is that very useful facility found on so many estates, an ice house. The mansion house, set on a hill above stone balustraded terraces and flanked by pavilions, is seen here in 1885 from the Italianate Gardens.

The number of staff required to service house and estate must necessarily have been large. Those "in service" tended to labour long hours meeting the daily requirements of the laird, his family and guests. Indeed, some devoted their whole lives to working in such a closed and restricted environment. I am reminded of some words displayed in the tearoom in Inverness Museum: *Mas leat an saoghal, is leat daoin' an domhain.* ('If the world is yours, the people of the

Belladrum House, Inverness-shire 5540

world are yours too'). No official could say who had written these words or explain them, but an interpretation could be that if you owned the land, then you also owned those who worked for you. Uncomfortably true, perhaps, for many working in the "big houses" before the First World War.

Down at the steading, I was told that in the hey-day of this estate the most vital part of one gardener's responsibilities was to supply the laird daily with a fresh carnation for his button-hole. At Belladrum one feels that could just be true!

Top: The Italianate Gardens, *c.*1910. Created in the 1850s, the gardens have sadly vanished. Although now grassed over, the round outline of the lily pond can still be traced.

Above: This part of Inverness-shire is very much "Lovat country" and Belladrum, which once formed part of the extensive Fraser lands. was sold to James Stewart in 1827. A subsequent owner, James Merry, who had made his fortune in the Lanarkshire coal and iron mines, engaged architect David Bryce in 1858 to remodel the existing house. The result, seen here, has been described as "the most elegantly built and furnished mansion house in the district, it is two stories high, slated and kept in the very best order". However, changing times and years of austerity following two world wars sounded the death knell for Belladrum which became a major financial liability. Although new uses were sought, none was found, and demolition took place in the late 1950s. Today, on the hill-top there is little trace of one of the county's most significant houses as Nature has largely reclaimed the site in the intervening years; only a small portion of a kitchen wing remains.

The Fraser ancestral line is a long one, the name being of Norman origin. At the height of their influence and power, Fraser-owned lands extended coast to coast across the breadth of Scotland from the Beauly Firth in the east to Mallaig and Morar in the west. The family crest is a buck's head and its motto is *Je suis prest*.

Clansmen and women had gathered to welcome them home following their honeymoon. Simon Joseph Fraser (1871-1933), 16th Lord Lovat, known as the Master of Lovat, is pictured here with his wife, the former Hon. Laura Lister, on the steps of Beaufort Castle on 5th November 1910. Lady Laura was a daughter of the 4th Lord Ribblesdale. Both images are photographic postcards, franked a few days after the event by Beauly Post Office and mailed by a Fraser to a fellow clansman in Minnesota, U.S.A.

Their son, Simon Christopher Joseph Fraser – later to become the 17th Baron – was born in 1911 and educated at Ampleforth School and Magdalen College, Oxford. Trained initially in the Scots Guards and the Lovat Scouts, he later transferred to No. 4 Commando and saw service in the raids on the Lofoten Islands and at Dieppe. He commanded the No.1 Special Service Brigade during the Normandy landings in June 1944 and was severely wounded. He stormed ashore at Sword Beach with his men and his personal piper playing *Blue Bonnets over the Border* as they engaged in the most bloody conflict imaginable. Piper Bill Millin's bagpipes, badly damaged by shrapnel, were given a permanent home in the National War Museum of Scotland in 2001. He died in 2010. Lord Lovat was a legendary and much decorated war hero who died in 1995, but it was the events that had taken place twelve months earlier which had such profound implications for the fortunes of Clan Fraser.

In March 1994, within the space of four days, a double blow struck totally unexpectedly as Lord Lovat's youngest and eldest sons both died in unrelated events – Andrew (the youngest) from injuries sustained on safari in Tanzania, and Simon from a heart attack while riding with the local hunt at Beaufort. For inheritance tax purposes Lord Lovat had handed over ownership of the estate many years previously to Simon who lived at the castle with his family. A rift was understood to have developed between the two in 1990 when Simon insisted on selling off 30,000 acres of prime deer forest and fishing rights – which he considered as uneconomic – for £15m. Worse was to come for it was only on Simon's death that the scale of his accumulated debts became apparent: they totalled £7.4m. This prompted a whole series of land disposals as the estate was broken up. Beaufort Castle, the adjoining home farm and about 800 acres were sold to Scottish businesswoman Ann Gloag who, with her brother Brian Souter, founded the Stagecoach bus company in 1980. Despite such damaging reverses, the Frasers retain a relatively modest acreage within the county, so that one can still refer legitimately to "Lovat country".

Beaufort Castle, *c.*1950. The present building dates from the 1880s and is believed to be the thirteenth building on this site. From every window there are magnificent views over the neighbouring countryside and the River Beauly. In 1937 the right-hand portion of the castle burnt down following a severe fire started in a chimney blocked by a bird's nest. The conflagration spread with terrifying speed and intensity, and was fought for ten hours by estate workers, volunteers, the Military and Inverness Fire Brigade. Meanwhile, hundreds of others removed valuable artefacts and paintings to safety from unaffected rooms in a race to beat the flames which had a firm hold before the fire brigade arrived. Another setback was that water pressure from the hydrants was low. The south wing and central tower were extensively damaged, and inevitably some valuable contents were lost. There was one fatality: a fireman fell off the engine hurrying from Inverness at the notorious double bend at Clachnaharry Bridge and sustained serious head injuries from which he died.

The 16th Baron raised the Lovat Scouts between 1899 and 1902 for service with the British Army and they initially saw action in South Africa during the Boer War. Recruited widely from the northern estates, these men excelled with horse and gun, and in fieldcraft – tracking, stalking and the like. Up until the First World War an annual camp was held, usually in June. Locations included Perthshire, Moray, Easter Ross and Skye, but this image shows them on the Beaufort Estate, their home ground. Souvenir postcards were specially produced for such camps, and the Post Office set up temporary local facilities to deal with the consequent mail.

AT THE OLD TOLL, BEAULY.   871

Beauly Toll lay just beyond Thomas Telford's Lovat Bridge of 1814 (and restored after flood damage in 1893), where the Strathglass Road joins the main highway one mile south of Beauly. In the early eighteenth century, turnpike trusts were created to repair and improve existing stretches of highway and to make new ones. The cost was raised by charging tolls, such roads being shut off with a "turnpike" (originally a revolving pole set with pikes, and later, a gate). Tolls were paid to the keeper whose toll-house stood beside the road. But he was more than a mere tax collector; he knew his patch well and often had knowledge of possible delays ahead – accidents, floods, snow-blocks or fallen trees. In the age of the horse-drawn coach other information, too, might be vital to coachmen, such as where the services of a local wheelwright or blacksmith might be obtained. Mishaps were all too frequent.

Top: Beauly Station, *c*.1910. Fifty years later, the stations beside the shores of the Beauly Firth at Bunchrew, Lentran, Clunes and Beauly were all closed. For those travelling north from Inverness today, the first really significant station reached is Dingwall, where lines diverge: westwards for Kyle of Lochalsh, and northwards to Thurso and Wick – both far-flung destinations which are properly regarded as Great Train Journeys.

Below: The First World War created an enormous demand for timber and forestry products which led directly to demands for improved forestry management and to the establishment of the Forestry Commission in 1919. This advertising card issued by Frank Sime, dated 28th January 1916 and addressed to Barber & Co (saddlers) in Inverness has the message: "Stock-taking. Please render your account, if any, up to and including January 31st, and let me have same not later than February 3rd, and much oblige".

FRANK SIME, TIMBER MERCHANT, BEAULY.

Upper Terminal of Ropeway, showing Loaded Carrier and Sawmill.

The Square, Beauly

Top: Plenty of activity in this scene looking south across Beauly Square, *c*.1890. The origins of human settlement in this corner of the Beauly Firth must reach back at least to the thirteenth century, when Beauly Priory was established. About 1805 Fraser of Lovat commenced building a planned estate village to which Thomas Strichen added designs for a square – more a rectangle – in 1840. Up to the end of Queen Victoria's reign cattle drovers came this way with their beasts on the way to the southern trysts, and cattle fairs were held here. Lord Lovat is said to have established the Caledonian Hotel (on the right) primarily for such men. The elevation of this image has led to some speculation that the photograph was taken from a window of the old Priory Hotel. *Above*: Looking north to the Priory Hotel and a tree which obscures Beauly Priory, *c*.1900. Note, extreme right, two ornate, distinctive pillar-mounted lamps marking the entrance to a substantial property on the corner of Ferry Road which once featured in so many old Beauly photographs. Now demolished, the "horribly suburban" architecture of the Royal Bank building *c*.1970 occupies the site.

This photograph of 1922 shows the Priory Hotel in ruins, awaiting demolition, following a major fire. In later years this part of the Square was landscaped and redeveloped to take on a new lease of life as the Beauly Centre, providing a shop, exhibitions and a tourist information centre.

Beauly Priory

4607

Beauly Priory, 1885. The origins of the name 'Beauly' are obscure. Beaulieu in Hampshire has a Cistercian abbey; the Anglo-Saxon form of Beo-lea became Beaulieu, the Bellus Locus Regis of the charters. Beaulieu was a name favoured by the Cistercians, perhaps as a tribute to their taste in choosing peaceful and picturesque locations for their religious houses. The Order originated from Citeaux (*Cistercium*), near Dijon having been founded in 1098 by Robert, Abbot of Molesme, under the strict observance of the Rule of St. Benedict. Of the several fraternities that evolved from the Cistercians, one was the Valliscaulian Order founded 1205 at Val des Choux (Valley of the Cabbages), Dijon. Beauly Priory was founded for this Order in 1230; its patron was initially Sir John Bisset of the Aird, and subsequently the Frasers of Lovat. Some twenty monks lived a life of austerity in contemplation and prayer, taking part in eight daily services; the regime commenced with Vigils at 3.30 a.m. and ended with Compline at 7.30 p.m. Study or work in the Priory grounds was allowed through the middle part of the day. By the early sixteenth century the fortunes of the community were in decline. Despite having been reformed as a Cistercian House with a newly-appointed abbot, hoped-for changes were short-lived. The Reformation Act of 1560 was the beginning of the end of the Priory's independence and shortly thereafter the religious house was abandoned.

Earlier reference was made to the Lovat Scouts Memorial. The inscription reads: "Erected by the Lovat tenantry and feuars of the Aird and Fort Augustus districts to commemorate the raising of the Lovat Scouts for service in South Africa by Simon Joseph, 16th Lord Lovat C.V O. C.B. D.S.O. who desired to shew that the martial spirit of their forefathers still animates the Highlanders of today and whose confidence was justified by the success in the field of the gallant corps whose existence was due to his loyalty and patriotism. A.D. 1905". On the west face, a bronze relief shows an officer looking through a telescope; a private steadies his horse. Panels around the base detail South Africa, Diamond Hill, Cape Colony and Wittebergen.

Beauly Square (East side). Old photographs show that the village always had a varied range of shops, just as it does today. The longest established business must surely be that of Campbell & Co (tailors and tweed mercers who number royalty among their customers). Their origins extend back to the 1850s, and their fame has spread far beyond Scotland. Note James McLean's grocery and provisions shop (left); he was also associated with a similar business at Tomich, Strath Glass. One particular aspect of the Square has changed however: there is vastly more traffic around today than in this image of c.1909.

Beauly and the meanderings of its river seen from the rising ground of Dunmore. The village is built over the orchards and gardens of the Priory, but the monks that settled here in the 13th century must have found this an agreeable site providing bounty from the fertile agricultural land, and salmon from the river. Little wonder it was their *bellus locus* .

Architects Matthews and Lawrie executed a large body of varied commissions across Inverness-shire, Ross-shire, Skye and North Uist. Mansions, courthouses, churches, schools, hospitals, banks and hotels all featured in their portfolio. In Beauly they were responsible for several buildings including, in the High Street, the Bank of Scotland and the Lovat Arms Hotel, both built in 1872. The hotel, a dignified, solid building, bears evidence of French Renaissance influence.

The brigantine *Van Righ* discharging cargo at Beauly Harbour, *c.*1908. Accumulations of silt and ever-changing shoals made navigation on the River Beauly a constant problem for mariners so that generally only vessels of modest tonnage, perhaps, up to 150 tons, put in here. In Victorian times, locally produced grain and cereals were exported, while coal and lime were brought in. About whether the piles of cut timber on the quayside are imports or exports we can only speculate, but the latter seems more likely.

SALMON LEAPING FALLS OF KILMORACK, INVERNESS-SHIRE.

The North of Scotland Hydro-Electric Board came into existence in 1943 following an Act of Parliament; the history of the Board is one of major engineering achievements which changed the face of parts of the Highlands. Hundreds of men worked on scores of power stations, tunnels and dams which in their sheer size and complexity were, and still are, regarded as giants of their time. There is no doubt that the generation of electricity has brought great benefit in its wake by raising living standards as well as providing power for industry, but we would deceive ourselves if it were not recognised that such progress has come at a significant cost to the environment – a matter to which I will return as we progress down Strath Glass, south of Beauly. The waters of the River Beauly (known as the River Glass in its upper reaches) were harnessed in a hydro-scheme completed in 1962 by the construction of dams and power stations, accompanied by the installation of Borland fish lifts to assist the spawning salmon, at both Kilmorack and Aigas. These images of the Kilmorack Falls taken 40 years previously gives some idea of their past attractions.

FALLS OF KILMORACK

302 KILMORACK WAR MEMORIAL, BEAULY

"We are the Dead. Short days ago we lived, felt dawn, saw sunset glow, loved and were loved, and now we lie in Flanders fields".

From *In Flanders Fields* by Lieutenant-Colonel John McCrae.

For those who have visited the First World War cemeteries of northern France and Flanders the experience is inevitably an overwhelming one, not only because they may be seeing the last resting place of a loved one, but the sheer scale of the human tragedy is so vividly revealed by the seemingly unending serried ranks of neatly maintained graves.

The largest armies the world had ever seen (before or since) had joined battle using new and enhanced weaponry, including the first ever use of deadly gas in a war theatre. The resulting casualties were horrific as tens of thousands of men were killed or maimed in a single day, often without a yard of territory gained. The landscape of Northern Europe over which they fought was shattered beyond description; conditions were appalling as incessant rain filled the trenches and shell craters, while the resultant mud slowed progress to walking pace. The blood, mud and attrition have ensured a special place in military history for what became known as The Great War.

Hostilities ceased at the eleventh hour of the eleventh day of the eleventh month in 1918. For the protagonists, after 51 months of unabated horror, the absence of the sound of gunfire somewhere seemed unnatural. Over time their emotions translated gradually from initial disbelief to uneasiness, eventually to profound relief – and finally for some, jubilation.

While no precise figure are available, there may be up to 100,000 war memorials ranging from cenotaphs, crosses and plaques in the British Isles. The Kilmorack War Memorial records the names of those from the surrounding straths and glens who flocked to embrace the course of action Britain had embarked upon in 1914, and had paid the ultimate sacrifice. Their deaths represent a staggering loss to this rural Highland parish which, as with those elsewhere, still casts an indelible shadow of grief right down to the present day. Those who returned were mentally scarred by what they had witnessed; for the remainder of their lives few would ever refer to their ordeal.

Aug. 3. 1903

This was taken shortly after that terrible accident at the Dhruim. Beauly. Many thanks for your card. It is very...

Among the items reported in *The Inverness Courier* of 3rd July 1903 were the opening of the Wick and Lybster Light Railway, the staging of an important Jacobite exhibition by the well-known firm of A. Fraser and Co. of Union Street, Inverness and a debate in the local Chamber of Commerce concerning motor cars being driven at excessive speed. Some things never change! Ominously, abroad there was worry over the possibility of serious trouble developing in the Balkans between Turkey and Bulgaria.

Headed "Traction Engine Accident, near Beauly – two men killed and one missing" a long report followed on the tragic events at the Dhruim, the gorge on the river at Kilmorack. A heavy traction engine towing two empty wagons was making its way from Beauly to the Erchless Estate to collect a quantity of timber for delivery to Beauly Station. Those involved in the ensuing drama were: –

James Sinclair (in charge of the vehicle), Donald Wemyss (his assistant), and Donald Mackenzie (steersman). En route they gave a lift to two other persons, Whyte and Fraser.

On the Strathglass Road, Sinclair allowed Wemyss to take control of the engine, while Mackenzie acted as "look out", and walked in front of the engine. Four miles south of Beauly, a halt was made at Teanassie to take on water and shortly thereafter it was noticed that water was escaping from a pump joint. Wemyss stopped the engine very close to a three-foot high wooden fence on the left-hand side of the narrow public road. Beyond the paling was a steep slope above the gorge which carries the river to the Falls of Kilmorack. Wemyss remained in charge of the vehicle while repairs were being carried out by Mackenzie.

Whyte went to sit in the first wagon; Fraser walked along the road and Sinclair sat on a nearby bank. The individual positions of these men would prove crucial in the events which unfolded.

In an effort to reposition the vehicle to allow traffic to pass, Wemyss put on full steam. The engine wheeled leftwards at speed, smashed through the wooden fence and careered down the slope towards the gorge. Both wagons had detached themselves before the engine plunged into the river. Mackenzie was first on the scene and went to seek medical help. Wemyss had terrible injuries and was dead; Whyte lay in great pain, unable to speak, and died subsequently on the way to the Northern Infirmary. Meanwhile, Sinclair melted into the background and disappeared – for two days – before being arrested. The resulting charges involved intoxication, being unfit for duty and allowing an inexperienced colleague to control the vehicle with the result that Wemyss and Whyte had been killed. He was committed to stand trial at Inverness on a charge of culpable homicide.

Many witnesses were called and all factors were discussed in detail including the wheel marks left by the swerving traction engine, the condition of the road and the actual parking position by the fence. The possible entanglement of a fence post with the rear wheel leading to the violent swerve to the left were all considered by the jury. After 55 minutes they returned to give a majority verdict of "not guilty". Sinclair was warmly congratulated by his supporters on leaving court. Surprisingly, perhaps, as the most experienced man it seems that he was not even censured for failing to come to the assistance of a dying man, or even go for help, having quitted the scene of a fatal accident.

CRASK OF AIGAS, STRATHGLASS   B 7742

Set amidst forests and grouse moors, Crask of Aigas, seen here about 1950, was built for those working on the Aigas Estate. Nearby, on either side of the road, are two locally significant properties. The older of these is Eileanaigas House situated on a small island in the River Beauly and a stronghold of the Frasers of Lovat since the 14th century. The house, dating from 1839 and subsequently enlarged, was built by Lord Lovat for the Sobieski-Stuart brothers who claimed to be related to Prince Charles Edward Stuart. They are recorded as a most talented and cultured pair having antiquarian interests. As Roman Catholics they attended chapel at Eskadale, sailing the short distance there from their island home by barge flying the royal standard from the masthead. They are buried at Eskadale.

*   *   *   *

On the hillside above the Strathglass Road, the baronial turrets of Aigas House, built to the designs of architects Matthews and Lawrie in 1877, can be glimpsed through trees. This 600-acre estate is presently the home of author and naturalist Sir John Lister-Kaye. Originally he had seemed destined for a life in industry, but in the late 1960s fate took him to the Isle of Skye to work with Gavin Maxwell, the author of *Ring of Bright Water*. Maxwell's intentions had been to establish a wildlife sanctuary on Eilean Ban ("the White Island"), otherwise known as Kyleakin Island, but his untimely death in 1969 put paid to the scheme, and in the process led a young Lister-Kaye to reassess his future prospects a second time. From his association with Maxwell sprang his next enterprise: the taking of field parties into the hills and the glens of Inverness-shire for the observation and study of wildlife. From this has developed his highly successful Aigas Field Centre which now attracts enthusiasts from afar to join escorted wildlife safaris across the Highlands.

Erchless Castle and Gardens, c.1905. While there can be no measure of absolute certainty, the likelihood is that the first Chisholm arrived in Britain from Normandy with William the Conqueror. However, there is little doubt that the clan's early powerbase was at Comar (Cannich) from where their lands around Glen Affric were controlled. Erchless Castle stands at the gateway to Glen Strathfarrar, and the Chisholms made their seat here early in the 17th century when the original tower-house was built. The chief of the clan was always referred to as "The Chisholm". The genealogy of the clan chiefs appears complex, but the direct line died out. In the burying-ground opposite the castle entrance are three Celtic crosses to one of the chiefs and his kin, near which are marble memorials to the Misses Mary and Annie Chisholm who died in 1927 and 1935 respectively – the last of the line. In common with the Frasers of Lovat who have vacated Beaufort Castle, The Chisholm no longer resides at Erchless. Moreover, his historic lands have been violated by the demands of hydro power generation, but saddest of all perhaps is that following the Clearances the clan was dispersed overseas resulting in more Chisholms being found today in Nova Scotia than there are in the silent, empty glens around Strath Glass.

The voices of conservationists, mountaineers and lovers of wild land were not heeded: rather like falling dominoes the glens of Affric, Cannich, and Strathfarrar fell one by one to the despoilers in the shape of the Hydro Board whose activities had been given legitimacy by an Act of Parliament in 1943. Post-war Britain needed electricity and these empty glens were regarded as prime targets, despite their being widely recognised as most magnificent examples of classic Scottish Highland scenery.

In Glen Strathfarrar, Beauly   95141 J.V

Temporarily we divert from the Strathglass Road at Struy Bridge, built by Thomas Telford in 1812, to take the narrow road inland through Glen Strathfarrar, pictured in 1925. The fifteen mile journey up to Loch Monar and its falls, and the view across the loch towards Strathmore, provided a microcosm of some of the very finest wild land, embracing hill, tree, river, loch and mountain scenery. Iain Thomson came this way in 1953 to become shepherd at Strathmore which could only be reached by boat having travelled the length of the loch. Surrounded by Munros – mountains over 3,000 feet – his cottage on the alluvial flats at Strathmore was more than just a little isolated as his neighbours throughout the whole glen numbered no more than a handful. Change came between 1960-2 as the Hydro Board pressed ahead with the scheme to dam Loch Monar; the first casualty was the road which was necessarily widened for construction traffic to build the horseshoe-shaped dam to contain the loch. Associated works throughout the glen included aqueducts, tunnels and two underground power stations. Massive change came in the wake of this new Highland "Clearance" as trees were felled and the few properties around the loch, including Thompson's, were burnt and then blown up. In just three months after completion of the scheme, Loch Monar had been enlarged by six miles and deepened by 100 feet. Thomson's book *Isolation Shepherd* is a classic of its type and a social document in its own right. It covers a phase in his life when he and the tiny community in the glen worked in harmony with Nature; more painfully it records the destruction of a way of life.

A chauffeur, with car at the ready, and domestic staff pose for this photograph outside Struy Lodge, c.1909. The estate has long been in the ownership of the Spencer-Nairn family, one of whom told me that the lodge was generally utilised for only a couple of months or so during the stalking season. There were about 40 bedrooms in the property which was a nightmare to run: winters could be harsh and in order to avoid burst pipes, radiators had to be filled on arrival and drained on leaving each season. However, this building was dismantled in the 1980s to be replaced by a modern single-storeyed house into which many of the internal doors and fittings from the earlier property have been incorporated. Inside, I was shown a picture of an even earlier lodge of 1880, confirming that at least three buildings have stood here.

The Beauly to Invercannich mail coach makes a stop at the Struy Inn, c.1900. Dating from 1896 the inn replaced an earlier hostelry, the Chisholm Arms, which stood nearer the river and which was the source of many old tales of the district. About this date, the "mail cart" left Beauly at about 2·30 p.m. and returned from Invercannich in time to catch the 9 a.m. mail at Beauly. Then, there was no road between Invercannich and Drumnadrochit.

Top: The scattered hamlet of Struy occupies both sides of the river. Turn left at the inn to join a minor road down Strath Glass for Cannich – a delightful alternative to our route, pictured here about 1920.

Middle: Known as Heather Cottages at the date of this image *c*.1905, the heather thatch was replaced with a slated roof about 1953. Earlier in their history the "old houses" were occupied by managers of the local working lead mine. In former times Struy could boast a carpentry and joinery business, a wheelwright, and a full working smithy.

Right: Strath Glass – geologically similarly formed as the Great Glen – but on a much more modest scale; the feature is well shown in this photograph.

STRATH GLASS, INVERNESS-SHIRE

Meanders of the River Glass through a wide alluvium-filled basin.   The valley is developed along a line of fault.

Geological Survey and Museum, London.   No. C. 1302.

The Holy Well of St. Ignatius, Strath Glass. Glassburn House nearby was built by Lord Lovat for a priest in this predominantly Catholic area, and the idea of a wayside well for the refreshment of travellers about 1880 may have been his. A draught of spring water can be collected from a stoup by means of a cup secured by a metal chain. Over the years the condition of the site has varied considerably, and a local resident told me that its maintenance generally depended on the interest displayed by successive owners of the house. The addition of a modern cairn commemorating royal events tends to sit uneasily with the picturesque, simple setting of the original shrine, seen here c.1935. But there is more than one saint bearing the name Ignatius; which one is dedicated here? I would suggest St. Ignatius of Loyola (1491-1556). He is known as the patron saint of soldiers whose Saint's day is 31st of July. He founded the Society of Jesus (the Jesuits) in the 16th century and was canonised in 1622 by Pope Gregory XV.

Cannich, c.1906. Rivers, glens and roads converge on this small hamlet which came to prominence after the Second World War as the hydro-electric schemes in Glen Affric and Glen Cannich were under construction. In 1951 the former was purchased by the Forestry Commission and regeneration of native woodland has been a prime objective, while parts of both glens were declared a National Nature Reserve by Scottish Natural Heritage in 2002. Within easy reach of Cannich both are "beautiful and dammed".

17 MILES FROM BEAULY.
14 MILES FROM TEMPLE PIER, LOCH NESS.
TELEGRAMS: "HOTEL, CANNICH."

GLENAFFARIC HOTEL !

CANNICH   BEAULY, N.B.

Above: The Glen Affric Hotel, another Matthews and Lawrie commission of 1862, looks very different today having been extended and re-faced about 1950 during the "hydro years" when the small indigenous population of Cannich was swollen by hundreds of labourers building the dams and associated facilities. Note the spelling on this early advertising postcard, referred to in the accompanying message: "Note the original spelling – as Gaelic is not a modern language, I would say I win on points, but of course that spelling would be before your time!". The initials NB, standing for North Britain, were frequently added to Scottish mail up to the First World War.

Below: A Macrae and Dick bus from Inverness outside the hotel in 1939.

GLEN AFFARIC HOTEL, GLEN CANNICH.   A.822.

In 1854 Dudley Coutts Marjoribanks, later Lord Tweedmouth, purchased the 22,000-acre Guisachan Estate – land long held by the Frasers whose ownership stretched back to the 15th century. The estate occupies the enchanting strath of Abhainn Deabhag where the wilder slopes of Kiltarlity and Affric meet the fertile pastures of upper Strathglass just south-west of Cannich. Tweedmouth, already a landowner in the Borders, was a countryman through and through, and fortunately had deep pockets as he had ambitious plans for his newly-acquired estate. He lost no time in clearing the glen of crofters and establishing the model village of Tomich for those displaced. A new mansion house would be needed together with a wide variety of estate buildings: farm steading, dairy, stables, factor's house, meal mill, laundry, kennels... the list seemed endless. No expense was spared and by about 1876 he had achieved most of his objectives and, you might think, laid the foundations for an enduring dynasty.

Top: Tomich House, originally a shooting lodge, later became the Tomich Hotel.

Centre: Post and Telegraph Office and General Merchant James McLean's Tomich branch of the Beauly business, 1910.

Bottom: Tenantry pose outside Guisachan Lodge and entrance gates to the 'Big House', c.1905.

Conservatory Guisachan.

GUISACHAN GARDENS.

J. McLERA TOMICH.

Above: Stairwell to the Billiard Room, flanked by marble cherubs and jardinières behind. The mural is a representation of the Caledonian Forest.

Centre: Lawns, neatly maintained flower-beds and ornate Victorian glasshouses. Following the break-up of the estate, the Forestry Commission owns the surrounding woodland. Some of the tallest Douglas firs in Scotland are to be seen, growing to over 65 metres in height.

Right: Huge courtyard farm steading of 1850/60 with clock-tower; the dairy has a decorative mosaic tiled floor. A number of vernacular buildings still stand and are in private ownership.

GUISACHAN HOME FARM, W. VIEW.

J. McLERA TOMICH.

Guisachan House, N. B.

GUISACHAN HOUSE, BEAULY.

McLEAN
CENTRAL DEPOT
BEAULY.

These images of the house show its setting and size. This tended to increase by extension at times co-incidental with highlights in Tweedmouth's political career: he served in the Administration of William Ewart Gladstone – four times Prime Minister of Great Britain and Ireland. Late 19th century publications feature the house interiors sumptuously filled with fine paintings, porcelain and furniture. Special features included "Wedgwood panels set into walls, mantelpieces and furniture which made the drawing-room unique". Wright and Mansfield, a famous London firm, was responsible for much of the decor. Visitors included the artists Millais and Sir Edwin Landseer, Mr. Gladstone and the Duke and Duchess of York (later King George V and Queen Mary) who must have been impressed with what they saw in this remote part of Inverness-shire. Some planted trees to commemorate their visit which still stand.

Guisachan's star was at its brightest during the Tweedmouth family ownership. The estate could boast valuable woodlands, a model farm with fine Highland and Aberdeen Angus pedigree cattle, and various breeds of dogs the most notable of which was the golden retriever, the very first of which was bred here. His Lordship certainly 'added value' in all he did, but the estate passed from family control in 1908. During the next 50 years, which included two world wars, a number of subsequent owners presided over the inexorable decline of the estate's fortunes: the size of the house had become a financial liability, and piecemeal sales had shorn the estate of income. Abandoned and unroofed in 1939, the stark ruins of today represent a small piece of history in suspension. Will a prince ever come this way again to reawaken this sleeping beauty? Most probably not. *Sic transit gloria mundi.*

MILTON, GLEN URQUHART. 200041 J.V.

East of Cannich, Temple Pier on Loch Ness lies fourteen miles distant by way of Glen Urquhart. At Corrimony in the 1950s, archaeologists excavated a chambered cairn, one of a number of passage graves found around the Inner Moray Firth, which they dated to 2000 B.C. Early Man must have seen Glen Urquhart as Arcadia: the River Enrick drains the glen through shallow Loch Meiklie, the hillsides are well-wooded even today, and the fertile valley floor was conducive to the raising of their animals and the cultivation of cereal crops. This 1926 image of Milton encapsulates the essential characteristics of the glen.

307/4 Public Hall Glenurquhart.

"This is to let you see the photo of Mrs Martin's hall erected for the pleasure of the people of the glen" is the message on this postcard of Glenurquhart Public Hall which was completed in 1906. There are few buildings that cement the social fabric of a small community better than a village hall, and many from the glen turned out when Mrs. Bradley Martin performed the opening ceremony that year. The generous benefactor was her husband, a wealthy American industrialist, who at that time held the tenancy of the 'Big House' of Balmacaan situated up the hill from Blairbeg where the hall is located.

Balmacan, Glen Urquhart

Valentines Series

THE DRIVE, BALMACAAN   1442

In the 1850s, the 7th Earl of Seafield decided to create a first class sporting estate at Balmacaan, the hub of the 50,000-acre Seafield Estates. In this 'age of improvement' something more impressive was required and the original modest property made way for this 40-bedroom mansion house. An American tycoon, Bradley Martin (1841 – 1913), took the tenancy from 1885 until his death, although his family returned every season until 1920. This period proved to be the high-water mark of the Balmacaan years as wealthy guests came to be waited upon by an army of "domestics" who catered for their every need. On hill and river a multitude of stalkers and ghillies would ensure their success with gun and rod.

But times were changing. In 1942 *Country Life* reported that the estate was to be offered for sale, either as a whole or in two parcels – Dochfour March to Loch Meiklie (15,000 acres) and Urquhart Castle to Balmacaan Forest (35,000 acres). By 1945 the actions of speculators had resulted in the break-up of the estate into 200 lots, of which the house was one. Balmacaan survived until 1972, neglected and extensively affected by dry rot when, following a demolition order, it was deliberately set on fire. A new property stands on the site today, and the road down to the village is much more overgrown than in this image, *c.*1910.

CASTLE URQUHART ☾M.R

Archaeological excavation suggests that Urquhart Castle stands on the site of an Iron Age fort. Early history is uncertain, but there is no doubt that whoever occupied this strategic and prominent stronghold above Loch Ness would control the Great Glen routes and the natural riches of Glen Urquhart. Clan rivalry and repeated conflicts between the armies of Scotland and England have seen much blood spilled here as they periodically wrested control from each other in the 13th and 14th centuries. Following reversion of the barony and castle to the Crown, King James IV gifted the Lordship of Urquhart to John Grant of Freuchie in 1509, conditional upon his undertaking the repair of the castle's fabric and building a range of domestic facilities within its walls. A further period of clan strife erupted in the 16th and 17th centuries causing structural damage, but after 1691 the castle ceased to be effective when much stonework was blown-up and dismantled to prevent possible Jacobite occupation. A severe gale in 1715 caused a partial collapse of the tower, beginning an era of deterioration in which stone was pillaged for use elsewhere. In 1912 the Trustees of the Seafield Estates transferred responsibility for the site to the State. For those requiring a comprehensive history, Historic Scotland maintains an excellent visitor centre.

Below: The Lower Ward from the Upper Ward, *c*.1920. Note the gatehouse (left); a range of domestic buildings including store, kitchen, hall and solar fronted Loch Ness.

3902. 14. Drumnadrochit.

Above: Harvesting at Drumnadrochit ("Hill-ridge by the bridge"), *c.*1906. In 1882 the Drumnadrochit Hotel (centre) arose on the site of an earlier inn whose stables can be seen alongside. The old hostelry had also previously doubled as local courthouse and Balmacaan Estate office. From the mid-1960s, the hotel expanded its tourist facilities by staging a permanent exhibition of Loch Ness and, of course, this included the history of the fabled monster and its sightings. The hamlet of East Balchraggan is on the hill, (top right).

Below: "Enjoyed an auto ride from Inverness to this place today. Beautiful scenery all the way alongside a lake" is the message on this postcard mailed to a relative in Newark, New Jersey and posted at Drumnadrochit Post Office (right) on 29th August, 1914.

No 005.   Drumnadrochit.

Post offices necessarily change locations for a variety of reasons. These two scenes may be of particular interest to local residents: the first postcard was mailed in August 1913, while the other showing Grant's Cash Stores is somewhat later.

Post Office, Drumnadrochit.

Post Office. Drumnadrochit

Viewville, looking West, Drumnadrochit.

Viewville, *c.*1920. This mid-Victorian villa with an attractive Italianate tower was once home of retired Balmacaan Estate factor, William Grant Stewart, who published *Songs of Glenurquhart*. Much later, and after substantial enlargement, Viewville became the Loch Ness Lodge Hotel.

Temple Pier lies on the north side of Urquhart Bay opposite the castle and it is thought to take its name from a nearby hostel once maintained by the Knights Templar. Originally a simple landing-place, the pier was built in 1854 on the re-opening of the Caledonian Canal in 1847 which brought vastly increased traffic: regular sailings by ships such as *Glengarry*, *Gairlochy* and *Gondolier* deposited mail, goods and tourists from Inverness, Fort Augustus and Banavie here, a mile east of Drumnadrochit. However, the growth of motor transport brought an end to such sea-borne traffic by 1929.

Temple Pier, Glen Urquhart.   John Murray, Post Office, Drumnadrochit.

John Cobb used the pier as his base while preparing to mount an attempt on the world water speed record in 1952. Sadly in September that year he lost his life when his boat, *Crusader*, broke up having attained a speed of 206 m.p.h. near the end of the first of two measured mile runs. Just south of Urquhart Castle at Achnahannet, a cairn stands by the roadside overlooking Loch Ness inscribed "a tribute to the memory of a gallant gentleman by the people of Glen Urquhart".

*   *   *   *

Along the length of the Great Glen Fault, there is a higher frequency of mild earth tremors recorded than anywhere else in Great Britain. Loch Ness is the largest of the glen's lochs at 24 miles long with a width of up to $1^1/_2$ miles, and holds more water than all the lakes in England and Wales combined. At the deepest point near Urquhart Castle, soundings have revealed depths approaching 1,000 feet; the temperature of the waters is fairly consistent and the loch never freezes over. But does a monster or a large sea creature exist here? Sightings are not new. In 565 A.D. disciples of St. Columba, the Irish missionary, recorded seeing a serpent in the River Ness which appeared on the surface "with a great roar and open mouth". Over the last two centuries many such sightings have been recorded in Scottish waters from Argyll to Orkney, and some 'sea-serpent experiences' have even been sworn under affidavit in Scottish courts. Discounting cases of mistaken identity and on occasions, outright fakery, there remains a very large body of accounts that are not easy to dismiss from individuals having the highest credentials and particularly where several people have witnessed an event simultaneously. The case for or against the existence of the Loch Ness Monster (*Nessum monstrosum*) is far from clear; best to keep an open mind perhaps...

*   *   *   *

"I was told at Lochend that the navvies have a tradition that Telford liked nothing better than to sit in the evenings with the navvies – hardy rough Highlanders they were, who had never been south – and smoke and chat with them over their drams".

Kilcumein and Fort Augustus,
Dom Odo Blundell O. S. B., 1914.

One often sees these days blithe references in the media concerning the so-called legacy of some politician or other; such claims are usually debatable, highly controversial, or even outrightly suspect. However, there can be no disagreement about the legacy of the man briefly portrayed here, for he conferred great benefit in so many ways throughout our island nation, and on the Highlands in particular. His name was Thomas Telford.

Telford was born in 1757, the son of a Dumfriesshire shepherd, and from these humble origins he rose to become the greatest civil engineer of his day. Early years found him labouring on local farms, building dry-stone walls and the like, but by the age of fourteen he was apprenticed to a stonemason. About 1780 he moved to Edinburgh where his acquired skills were in great demand as the New Town was being developed. Within a couple of years he was in London working on Somerset House and subsequently on the dockyard at Portsmouth. During this

Thomas Telford.

period, his enquiring mind and meticulous attention to detail brought him to the notice of Sir William Pulteney, through whom he became appointed surveyor of public works for Shropshire in 1787. There, while continuing his studies on a range of subjects bearing on his professional work, he became involved in a great variety of works which led the development of his future career into civil engineering. He demanded high standards and possessed an incredible aptitude for every detail and aspect of the work on which he was engaged, whether it was building, designing or engineering. He was held in high regard, not only by all those with whom he came into contact, but also by his workmen, with the result that many of the best moved with him around the country from project to project. He excelled at working in difficult terrain where he produced innovative solutions.

Thomas Telford's lifetime achievements were prodigious. He either cut or was associated with many important canals, the building of over 1,000 miles of road (including London to Holyhead) and the development of more than thirty harbour and dock schemes which included St. Katherine's Docks in London and others in Aberdeen, Dundee and Pultneytown (Wick). There are also over 1,200 bridges to his credit – among them five across the River Severn, the Menai Suspension Bridge, Conway Bridge, Dean Bridge (Edinburgh) and Broomielaw Bridge (Glasgow).

The construction of the Caledonian Canal flowed indirectly from Telford's appointment as Surveyor to the British Fisheries Society in 1796. Five years later he was instructed by the Treasury to select sites for fishing stations on the Scottish West Coast, to plan safe communication between the mainland and the islands and to investigate the possibility of a canal between the west and east coasts. The idea of a waterway running the length of the Great Glen was not new as James Watt had made a survey in 1773, but the promoters abandoned that scheme on grounds of cost (then £164,031 exclusive of the land). Telford's survey and his estimated costs of £497,531 was accepted, and construction commenced in 1804.

While the total length of the waterway is 60½ miles, only twenty-two of these are constructed canal. This, the first state-aided transport system in British history involved the building of twenty-nine locks, ten bridges and four aqueducts. The highest point is Loch Oich with Laggan Reach at 106 feet above high water at Inverness.

Technical difficulties occasioned delays. These included a porous lock at Fort Augustus, the flight of locks at Banavie known as 'Neptune's Staircase' which took four years to complete, while at Corpach navvies had to cut the basin out of solid rock by hand. Little wonder perhaps, that the whole project came out somewhat over budget at £905,258, and that subsequent expenditure on remedial work in the years up to 1847 brought the accumulated cost to £1¼ million.

When opened in 1822 the canal, at fourteen feet deep, was found not to be satisfactory, and a four-year closure between 1843 and 1847 enabled deepening and modifications to be made leading to a triumphal re-opening. But the canal never lived up to the expectations of its protagonists and, even before the work had been completed, there were regrets that it had not been undertaken on a grander scale. There were other factors too, as the world had moved on: the shadow of the Napoleonic threat had been lifted, the Baltic timber trade had collapsed, the building of coastal lights had diminished the dangers of the Northern Passage but, above all, steam and much larger vessels were fast replacing sail.

Telford no doubt witnessed such trends as the viability of his canal was questioned, although his death in 1834 spared him from witnessing their confirmation. Nonetheless, the construction of a waterway which split the Highlands in two was a remarkable achievement, bequeathing an asset much used today, especially for pleasure and tourism purposes.

Upon his death, he was honoured by a grateful nation with interment in Westminster Abbey. His huge, varied and quite exceptional legacy throughout the land stands as a testament to his skill, energy and perseverance which endures to this day.

Right: The Caledonian Canal at Dochgarroch, four miles from Inverness, 1920. Passengers on the P. S. *Gondolier* crowd forward to witness a little canalside entertainment. A crew member and the lock-keeper are assisted by a boy and, somewhat uniquely, by a dog to work the capstan by which the lock gate will open. Hydraulic power has now replaced the manual exercise shown here which took seven revolutions to open and close the gates.

Dochgarroch Loch: Dog Opening Gate

CALEDONIAN CANAL AND TOMNAHURICH.

Above and right: The sweep of the canal at Tomnahurich and the hilltop cemetery. The hill in the background, shaped like an upturned boat, is nearly 200 feet high and a place where many of the great and good of Inverness are interred. Reached by a zigzag drive, even the top of the hill has been adapted by levelling to accommodate tombstones. The site is considered to be of great beauty and is famed for its monuments and the extensive views from the hilltop.

Tomnahurich Cemetery, Inverness

Inverness - Arrival of Steamer at Muirtown.

Afternoon arrival at Muirtown, Inverness, *c.*1905. Across the Highlands and Islands the arrival of any steamer was always a significant event, and no less so at this important tourist interchange. There must have been a sense of anticipation as passengers swarmed across the wharf to the line of horse-drawn omnibuses waiting to whisk them into the Highland capital. Some will have telegraphed ahead to pre-book accommodation, while others will make an on the spot selection from the wide variety of hotels and boarding-houses available locally. Those who had spent the night at the Lochiel Arms Hotel at Banavie (near Fort William) and boarded the *Gondolier* after breakfast will have spent eight leisurely hours on the 60-mile waterway and savoured a feast of sights and shared experiences with others joining the boat at various locations along the way.

The P. S. *Gondolier* is the steamer most readily associated with the Caledonian Canal as she operated on this route for over 70 years. Built in 1866, reports of the period refer to her elegance and comfortable appointments. We will meet her elsewhere in this book, but meanwhile will rejoin those tourists who have just arrived at Muirtown as they make their way into Inverness.

Inverness   *Arrival of Passengers*

INVERNESS

Inverness – the mouth of the Ness, derived from the Gaelic term INBHIR ("mouth"). Geographical factors have influenced the growth and wealth of this town from earliest times and unsurprisingly perhaps, shipbuilding was an early industry here. From all points of the compass, land and sea routes naturally converge around the sheltered Inner Moray Firth bringing travellers and trade together; on that account alone, Inverness was destined to play a significant role in the life and history of the Highlands and of the Scottish nation. Earliest history is obscured in the mists of time. Learned authorities believe that the legendary 14th King of Scotland, Evenus II, founded the town; he died about 60 B.C. However, one particular date emerges with clarity, that of 565 A.D. when St. Columba is recorded as having visited Inverness following his landing on Iona *c.*563. King David I and William the Lion, King of the Scots, both granted royal charters; in fact, the latter granted four, and by that of 1180, the King agreed to make a fosse around the town which the burgesses were to enclose with a good paling. The history of the Highland capital is a long and eventful one, and further historical references have necessarily been confined to particular aspects of the images which follow.

Caledonian Canal steamer sailings commenced and terminated at Muirtown Wharf above a flight of four locks. Mrs Laing's hotel by Muirtown Bridge at the top of Telford Street was located within a stone's throw of this landing-stage and conveniently placed for those visiting Muirtown and Clachnaharry. However, the great majority of those arriving by the *Gondolier* were quickly aboard the waiting omnibuses and heading down Fairfield Road into Inverness to arrange their accommodation. Of the larger hotels on the west bank of the River Ness were the Alexandra, Palace and Glenalbyn, while across the suspension bridge in the town centre were rather grander edifices – the Station, Royal, Waverley and Caledonian, all within easy reach of the railway station.

For such tourists an excellent pocket-sized guide to Inverness was available, priced two pence (2*d.*). The 1907 version included a street plan, a short history and advertisements for shops and services that none should miss. There were suggestions of what to do, where to go and what to see, and if a copy had not already been purchased aboard the *Gondolier*, those visiting the Highland capital for the first time would have been well-advised to secure a copy immediately.

The Palace Hotel, on the west bank of the River Ness opposite the castle, was built in 1890 and claimed at one time to be "nearest to the canal steamers". Such claims were often short-lived and stolen by other hotels which sprung up nearby to meet tourist demand.

INVERNESS
The Palace Hotel

Beautiful, quiet situation on the banks of the River Ness, opposite the Castle.

Electric Light.   Garage.   Terms Moderate.

In 1930, the Caledonian Hotel in Church Street was in the proprietorship of Frank Steven whose advertisements emphasised the location as within one minute's walk of the railway station and continued, "This well-known first class hotel – patronized by Royalty – is the largest and best appointed hotel in town, and universally acknowledged one of the most comfortable in Scotland. The view from the windows is unsurpassed, showing miles of mountain scenery and overlooking the River Ness. Headquarters of the A.A. and R.S.A.C. Hotel porters meet all trains and convey luggage to and from the station free of charge". This postcard *c*.1920, has the message, "This is the river side of our hotel; they are expecting 150 journalists from London this evening – a special train bringing them".

Caledonian Hotel from the River, Inverness

Above: Travellers from the north and those arriving on the canal steamers would have entered town through these portals, crossing the river by the graceful suspension bridge built 1850–55 at a cost of £26,000; it survived until being replaced in 1961. The rose-coloured sandstone battlements of the modern castle built in Victorian times house the County Buildings and Court House, replacing the Hanoverian fortress blown-up by the Jacobites in the "Forty-Five"; of that castle only a deep well and part of a bastion wall remain. This site has been a stronghold since the 12th century. The blend of architectural proportionality so evident in 1900 is sadly not reflected in the same view from Huntly Street today.

Below: The British Empire Exhibition of 1924–25 was a celebration of the history, science, industry, arts and culture of Britain and its Dominions, Colonies, Dependencies and Protectorates. The sheer scale and magnitude of the 216-acre Wembley site – which included the new football stadium – had echoes of the Great Exhibition of 1851. The exhibition emblem was the lions of Wembley, and over the two years 27 million people attended. In the stadium on 23rd April 1924, King George V declared the exhibition open before a crowd of 110,000 people. The broadcasting of the opening ceremony by the BBC, founded only 18 months previously in October 1922, was considered a triumph. Many public venues installed loudspeakers, and in theatres, shops and open spaces, large crowds assembled to listen, as here at Inverness Castle. Today we take all this for granted, but in 1924 wireless telegraphy was a relatively new science with which the name of Guglielmo Marconi (1874 – 1937) is forever linked. He had begun experimenting with radio waves in 1894, was granted a patent for radio transmissions three years later, and successfully supervised the sending of the first radio signals across the Atlantic between Poldhu (Cornwall) and Newfoundland in December 1901.

The changing face of Bridge Street. An ever-increasing volume of traffic resulted in the attractive portal to the suspension bridge being demolished.

Queen Mary's House, Inverness.

Although modernised, much of the curious old structure still remains. The walls are of great thickness. Around Queen Mary the loyal clans of Munro, Fraser and Mackenzie were gathered under Lord Lovat. Prince Charlie took up his residence here in 1746. The Steeple of the old Jail 130 feet in height was built in 1791.

Right: Queen Mary's house, *c.*1900. Said to be the house where Queen Mary lived in 1562 prior to gaining admission to the castle, the Official Inverness Guide of 1930 detailed this as a very old building above a series of stone and lime vaults, having massive walls five feet thick. Be that as it may, but this did not prevent demolition some 30 years later. Many fine buildings have been lost to the town since 1950.

High Street, Inverness   Valentines Series

High Street, *c.*1890. The sculptures of Faith, Hope and Charity adorning the balustrade atop the Tartan Warehouse have long vanished; the Forbes Fountain (centre) gifted by Dr. G.F. Forbes of Millburn about 1882 has since been relocated, minus canopy, to Ladies Walk.

CLACHNACUDDIN AND TOWN CROSS, INVERNESS.

Right: The Town Cross, a blend of stonework cannot be satisfactorily or uniformly dated, while the Clach-na-cudainn Stone (spellings vary) embedded at its foot has seen several locations before finding a resting-place here. If tradition is to be believed, the bluish stone has a long association with Inverness, for centuries having some ceremonial use or acting as an omen of good fortune. At one time residents carrying tubs of water from the Ness to their homes often rested them on the stone – hence the name, "stone of the tubs".

Far right: A menu produced for the tourist trade!

SCOTCH MENU.

Some hae meat and canna eat, | But we hae meat an' we can eat,
An' some wad eat that want it, | Sae let the Lord be thankit.

SOME O' THE THINGS WE'LL HAE—

SOUPS.
Sheep's Heid Kail.   Cockie-Leekie.   Hen Bree, an' a Dram.

FISH.
Cauld Saumon.   Troots.   Tawties an' Herrin'.
Anither Dram.

HAGGIS WI' A' THE HONOURS.
"Fair fa' your honest sonsie face,
Great chieftan o' the puddin' race!"
Sic a grand nicht we're haein'.   We'll hae anither Mouthfu'.

JOINTS.
Sautit Soo's Leg Biled.   Gigots o' Mutton Roasted.
Laich Cuts o' Beef Roasted.
Peas.   Ingans.   Tawties, biled and champit.
Bashed Neeps, an' ither Orra Vegetables.   Anither Dram.

ENTREES AND ORRA DISHES.
Roast Bubblyjocks Stuffed.   Roasted Jucks.   Stoved Hens.
Doo Pie.   Trumlin Tam.   Heck! Anither Tastin'.

DESSERT AN' SICLIKE.
Grozet Tairt.   Apple Tairt.   Rhubarb Tairt.   Baps.
Bakes.   Ait Cake in Fars.   Parleys.   Scones.   Snaps.
Curran' Loaf wi' Raisins intilt.   Shortbread wi' Raisins on't.
Curds an' Cream.   Glesca Jeeline an' ither Trifles.
Ma certie, we'll hae anither Dram.
Kebbucks, green an' Mitey.

WINES.
Toddy.   Scotch Toddy.   Hielan' Toddy.   Athol Brose.
Strong Yill.   Barley Bree frae weel-kent Scottish Vineyards.
We're no that fou.   An' we'll tak' a Cup o' Kindness yet.

For Teetotal Folk an' siclike, we'll hae Claret (which some folk ca'
Soordook), Cuddle ma' Dearie, Skeichan, Treacle Yill, an' ither Drinks
o' that ilk, New Maskit Tea, etc.

INGLIS STREET, INVERNESS 525

Above: A busy scene in the 1920s. Inglis Street provided a short link between High Street and the town's principal commercial centre surrounding Academy Street and the railway station.

THE WASHINGTON
TEMPERANCE HOTEL,
HAMILTON STREET,
INVERNESS.

Facing High Street, and within Two Minutes walk from Station.

Miss C. MACKAY,
Proprietrix.

Tariff.

Bed, from.... ....1s. 6d.

Breakfasts and Teas.............1s. 3d. to 2s.

Dinners, from..................................1s.

Attendance....................................1s.

Lemon's Ærated Waters, per bottle........3d.

Boots attend Trains and Steamers.

Left: Front and back of a Victorian trade card for Miss Mackay's Temperance Hotel in nearby Hamilton Street.

Standing directly opposite Inverness Station across Academy Street, the Royal Hotel was flanked by Union Street and the three distinctive arches of the Market Arcade. Built in the 1860s and re-fronted in 1873, the Royal was for much of its existence in the ownership of the Christie family and later Trust House Hotels Ltd. – a well-regarded company owning 200 hotels across the length and breadth of Britain. In 1885, J. J. Christie wrote, "The public rooms, private sitting-rooms and bedrooms are large, lofty and furnished throughout in the handsomest manner possible, and no expense has been spared to make this hotel one of the best, as it is one of the quietest and most comfortable in Scotland".

Christie was an avid collector as evidenced by these Victorian images of the drawing-room and entrance hall which, together with other public rooms were packed with fine furniture, glass and porcelain; guests may have wondered whether they had strayed into a museum! Trust House Hotels were subsequently subsumed by the Forte Group, and the building is currently the offices of the Clydesdale Bank.

THE DRAWING ROOM, ROYAL HOTEL, INVERNESS.

ROYAL HOTEL, INVERNESS.

The shops and stalls of Inverness Market have provided a shopping experience under one roof for residents and tourists alike since the development of the complex 1890–7 which gave access from Academy and Union Streets and from Queensgate.

If Inverness has a hub then it is surely Station Square where cabbies and their patient horses await train arrivals from all parts of Scotland, *c.*1895. In the foreground, the Cameron Highlanders Monument built of Portland stone was unveiled by Cameron of Lochiel in 1893. Either side of the station entrance are the headquarters of the Highland Railway (left) and the Station Hotel, built in the 1850s. The adoption of a change of name in recent years has offended some, but 'the Station' and Robbie's Bar within it is a major institution and many continue to use the original name. When the hotel first opened its doors 150 years ago, pianos were at the disposal of guests having private sitting-rooms at no extra charge, but a cold bath would add a shilling (1/-) to the bill.

The development of Inverness as a railway interchange was a natural consequence of its geographical location. The line to Nairn – later extended to Aberdeen – commenced in 1855; several Highland lines subsequently converged here, and the direct route south to Perth and beyond opened in 1898.

Above: The arrival of an overnight train from London about 1906.

Below: Victorian buildings such as this huge arch were often constructed to a monumental scale and intended to last; this one, unsurprisingly, was known locally as "Marble Arch". Engines passed through here from the coaling stage on their way to the "Roundhouse". This was a series of engine sheds grouped around a turntable where rolling-stock awaited their next call of duty. One such engine is seen in Bay 31, *c.*1905.

UNION STREET, INVERNESS 523

Opposite the railway station, Union Street connects Academy Street with Church Street. Laid out in 1863, this thoroughfare and the surrounding area quickly became established as the town's principal commercial centre. Above the shops (right), windows of the Royal Hotel look down on a wide variety of businesses in this late 1920s scene. In the background the skyline is broken by a tower of the Caledonian Hotel in Church Street, while alongside, the Canadian Government Immigration Office can be seen. For 250 years Highlanders have been forced overseas to seek new opportunities in periodic waves of emigration prompted by the infamous forcible evictions of the Clearances, the repression which followed in the aftermath of the 'Forty-Five' and during periods of severe unemployment which continued into the 20th century. The purpose of such facilities here in the Highland capital would have been to explain the formalities and make information available to those intent on leaving their native land – an act of great reluctance and something never lightly undertaken.

Beyond the street lamp (left) was the large store of A. Fraser & Co. – literally a household name for more than a century across the Highlands where they were renowned as "Complete House Furnishers, Estate Agents and Auctioneers". This 1930 advertisement shows their business activities knew no bounds, even embracing a museum! This particular advertisement has a significance to which I will make later reference.

An original piece of stationery showing the Waverley Hotel posted to Miss Dickinson of 116 Blackman Lane, Leeds in January, 1907. The Waverley claimed to be "unsurpassed for situation and comfort, combined with moderate charges. Hot and cold water in principal bedrooms. Porter of hotel attends all trains".

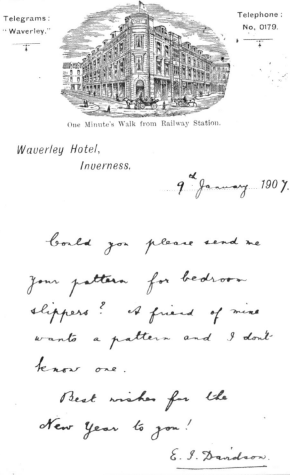

These days Barclays Bank operates from 19 Union Street, but when this photograph was taken in September 1923 the Royal Bank transacted business there. The staff are identified as:

Back row: Mr. Morrison (Accountant), Mr. Cameron (New Agent)
Front row: T. Owens, E. R. Fraser (Teller), W. D. McPhail,
     A. Kyle Forsyth, Mr Cargill (Retired Agent).

A policeman and several passers-by observe the cameraman closely as he clicks the shutter to take this Church Street scene in the 1920s. In a distance of approximately 300 yards along Church Street to Friars Street there are no less than seven churches. The graveyard in Friars Street is the site of a 13th century Dominican Friary founded by Alexander II, and much of the surrounding area must have been hallowed ground from an early date, so perhaps the statistic is less surprising than might initially appear.

On the west side of Church Street is Abertarff House built in 1593 as the town residence of Fraser of Lovat and now the last surviving example of the old turnpike stairs – once a common feature in the town's domestic architecture.

Below: A 1907 advertisement for John Macpherson's shop at 24 Church Street which catered specifically for sportsmen. Hunting, shooting and fishing are of great economic importance throughout the Highlands. Success on hill or river could be crowned by having your fine trophy stuffed for mounting at home to impress your friends.

The old Dunbar
Hospital.
INVERNESS.

1646.

Dunbar's Hospital, Church Street, *c.*1900. Provost Alexander Dunbar built this almshouse in 1668 using, it is said, materials from the demolished Citadel in Cromwell Road. He endowed the building as a Grammar School, Weigh House and Hospital for the poor under the care of the Old High Kirk Session. As can be seen, more than a century ago, part of the premises were let, presumably to produce rent; over the round-arched entrance there is an heraldic stone of 1676 with an accompanying inscription stipulating that rent from the Weigh House was to be paid to the Hospital's treasurer.

An advertisement of 1930.

PROPRIETOR AND MANAGER - - MR CAMERON BURGESS.
ACTING MANAGER - - MR EDWARD TODD.
CONDUCTOR OF ORCHESTRA - - MR HARRY T. TUFF.

HOLDS, at ORDINARY PRICES, £60,

Viz. : Circle, **3s**; Stalls, Side and Upper Circles, **2s**; Pit, **1s**;
Gallery, **6d.**

Proscenium Opening, 19 ft. ; Depth of Stage, 28 ft. ; Size of Cloths,
24 x 20 ft. in height. Six Dressing Rooms, &c.

Doors Open at 7.30. Curtain at 8 p.m.

Booking Office—Messrs LOGAN & CO., of Inverness, Ltd.,
Musicsellers, Church Street.

In 1881 several private individuals formed a company for the purpose of building and equipping a theatre for the town. A suitable site was found on Bank Street close to the Old High Church; the later development of the Free North Church in 1893 saw the theatre dwarfed by competing spires either side of it. Architects Matthews and Lawrie were instructed to prepare detailed plans. These included a circular auditorium with seating for 750, together with the usual private boxes, stalls, side and upper circles, pit and gallery. Opening night on 6th November, 1882 was a great success attended by a large, appreciative audience who were greatly impressed by the facilities and the night's performance. It was an auspicious beginning: the Theatre Royal went on to establish itself firmly in the artistic life of the town – that is at least to March 1931 when disaster struck around 1 a.m., several hours after the conclusion of an evening performance. The fire was fierce and spread rapidly through the building, but by pumping water from the river the Fire Brigade prevented adjoining buildings being engulfed. When the roof collapsed, the "Royal" was reduced to a mere shell with the loss of all contents; only the safe containing that night's takings and Tom, the theatre cat, survived the inferno. This rare item written and signed by Cameron Burgess (Proprietor) was mailed on 9th December, 1910.

D. WHYTE, PHOTOGRAPHER,

Whyte, Photographer.

55 & 57, Church Street, INVERNESS.

Patronised by H.M. The KING and Nobility of the North.

8

The Whyte Collection consists of over 100,000 photographic images and was acquired by The Highland Photographic Archive 80 years after the death of photographer David Whyte in 1905 at the age of sixty-two. The collection came courtesy of Mr F. Hardley who was the last of successive proprietors of Whyte's former studios at 55/57 Church Street. Many of the earliest items suffer from a lack of documentation and, where it does exist, often consists of no more than a name scratched on a glass plate. A native of Ayr, Whyte had come to Inverness in the early 1860s and established his first studio in Greig Street, later moving to Union Street before settling in Church Street where he purchased the photographic business of Collier and Park. As a photographic artist he was known across the Highlands, and obituaries testify to the high regard in which he was held. His photographs included leading Highland families, distinguished visitors and members of the Royal Family. Most likely, this image of His Majesty King Edward VII was taken at Glenquoich in 1904. (Advertisement, Christopher J. Uncles Collection. © the Highland Photographic Archive, Highland Council.)

Seasonal scenes on the Islands, River Ness. An Edwardian concert by visiting musicians provides summer season entertainment. By way of contrast, this is paired with a late Victorian winter landscape. "The Islands: these are three in number, and are connected by footbridges. They derive their chief beauty from the splendid trees and shrubs which grow upon them. Glorious beeches overhang the water; oak, ash, fir and hazel all thrive, and amongst the shrubs the rhododendron is conspicuous, while the ground in places is carpeted with bluebells". *Thorough Guide Northern Highlands*, M. J. B. Baddeley, 1884.

A 1930 town guide describes that at nightfall the Islands are transformed into a sylvan fairyland, "lit up by festoons of tiny lamps glittering amongst the foliage, and with innumerable electric lights and Chinese lanterns suspended along the avenues of stately trees, the scene presented to the eyes of the spectator is unique in its entrancing beauty". However not everyone agreed: the celebrated traveller and author H. V. Morton described the scene as "regrettable" after a visit in the late 1920s!

On the Islands, Inverness (Winter)

South Kessock, *c.*1900. North Kessock lies under Ord Hill along the Black Isle shore just ¹/₂ mile across the firth; that fact alone ensured that this was a ferrying-place from earliest times. Before the age of mass transport, some Black Isle residents would row themselves across to visit Inverness as this saved a time-consuming journey around the head of Beauly Firth. As volumes of traffic increased throughout the 20th century, the ferry-boat was progressively upgraded to cope with demand, and a vehicular ferry plied the route until the building of the Kessock Bridge in 1983 made the service redundant.

Longman Aerodrome, 29th May 1934. The new air mail service between Inverness and Orkney was inaugurated when the air mail pennant was presented. On the platform were, left to right: Provost Mackenzie, Sir Frederick Williamson (Director of Postal Services), Captain E. E. Fresson OBE and Mr. Campbell. On 30th May over 2,000 letters were carried from Inverness to Kirkwall with 12,000 being carried on the return flight. Another page in our postal history had been written for this was the first internal air mail service in Britain. Captain Fresson had formed Highland Airways Ltd. the previous year, and the first scheduled flight took place on 8th May from Inverness to Wick and Kirkwall with a four passenger twin-engined monoplane. These early air services expanded, bringing benefits to small communities, and his pioneering work was commemorated by the unveiling of a memorial to him at Kirkwall Airport in 1976. (Star Photos of Perth).

These two unusual postcards of 1906 bear the imprint of Alexander's Book and News Agency of Inverness and are advertisements for two newspapers, both Highland institutions in their own right – *The Inverness Courier* and the *Highland News*. The newsprint is portrayed torn aside to reveal little cameos of the castle and the River Ness. *The Inverness Courier and General Advertiser* as it was then named expressed its catchment area as "the counties of Inverness, Ross, Cromarty, Nairn, Moray, Sutherland and Caithness", while the *Highland News* was content with: "Eight pages – price one penny". The cost of the *Courier* was the same.

Back in 1906 in an age long before radio and television, most received news and information by word of mouth or newspapers, and the press barons at national and local levels fought hard to retain readership and increase circulation (not too dissimilar from today!).

In those far-off days the *Courier* and the *News* were rivals and fiercely independent, but today both newspapers operate under the banner of the Scottish Provincial Press Ltd. That company has a portfolio of titles across the Highlands, all still functioning under their historic names and providing an excellent news-gathering service relative to their 'patch'. While pursuing enquiries relating to aspects of research over the years, my experience in making contact with various editors and journalists has been wholly worthwhile having yielded information of a local nature which would otherwise have been difficult to obtain.

The Inverness Courier celebrated its 150th anniversary as far back as 1967, and an even more important landmark is not too far distant. Despite the ever-increasing challenges faced by the industry, and the new and different ways in which news can be accessed today, let us hope that local newspapers countrywide continue to play a vital role within their communities.

The curving peninsulas at Fort George and Chanonry Point virtually overlap to enclose within their pincer-like formation the Beauly and Inner Moray Firths, thus creating a large area of relatively sheltered water. From earliest times shipbuilding was an Inverness industry, although the harbour proper (seen here c.1913) was developed from the mid-seventeenth century. Thomas Pennant, who had visited Inverness in 1769, noted in his *Tour of Scotland* that, "the present imports are chiefly groceries, haberdasheries, hardware and other necessaries from London: and of late six to eight hundred hogsheads of porter are annually brought in. The exports are chiefly salmon, those of the Ness being esteemed of more exquisite flavour than any other. Herrings, of an inferior kind, taken in the Firth from August to March… The commerce of this place was at its height a century or two ago, when it engrossed the exports of corn, salmon and herrings, and had besides a great trade in cured codfish now lost, and in those times very large fortunes were made here". By 1930 the harbour had been upgraded, Coast Lines Ltd. was operating a regular steamer service, accelerating the position of the town as the premier distribution centre for northern Scotland. Close to Thornbush Quay were the slipway and shipbuilding yard of the Rose Street Foundry and Engineering Company which specialised in the building and repair of steam drifters.

The clock tower in Cromwell Road pictured here c.1900, and now surrounded by modern port facilities, is all that remains of the large pentagonal Cromwellian Fort built between 1652 and 1658, and known as the Citadel. The stronghold for 1,000 men and 600 horse was constructed to a height of three storeys with hewn stone, which various accounts detail as having been pillaged from Beauly Priory, Fortrose Cathedral and Kinloss Abbey. The great gate to the north, named the Port, included a strong oak drawbridge and a wide moat enabling boats to sail in at high tide. To the south, a sallyport led to the town. Two years after the Restoration of 1660 the garrison was withdrawn and the Citadel, which had so briefly become a local landmark, was dismantled at the express demands of some of the Highland chiefs.

*   *   *   *

Victorian and Edwardian tourists will have experienced many of the scenes shown in this section of the book. However, before returning home, there was one particular place that many felt drawn to and that lay just five miles from town…

CULLODEN AND LOCH NESS (EAST)

In the 18th century two attempts were made to effect a Stuart Restoration. Mary of Modena, second wife of King James II of England gave birth to James Edward Francis, Prince of Wales (commonly called the Old Pretender), and an unsuccessful attempt was made by the Jacobites, or Stuart party, to set this prince on the throne by force of arms in 1715. Thirty years later his son, Prince Charles Edward Stuart (right) – known as Bonnie Prince Charlie or The Young Pretender – made a more determined effort to seize the crown. Landing on the west coast of Scotland with a handful of followers, he gained the allegiance of several Highland chiefs, raising his standard on 19th August 1745 at Glenfinnan where a force of 1,200 clansmen committed themselves to his cause. Over the ensuing months an extraordinary series of military engagements, and not a little luck, brought the Jacobite army, now numbering 5,000, as far as Derby: a monument there marks the southernmost point of their advance, just 120 miles from London. Consternation reigned in the capital where the military was hastily marshalled to counter the insurgents, but they now had problems of their own. Extended supply lines through England, where there was minimal support for the insurgency, physically tired by the long march south, riven by differences on strategy and the failure of foreign assistance to materialise, were all factors which culminated in a decision to retreat to Scotland. Inverness, the Highland capital where Jacobite sympathies were strongest had to be defended at all costs. The retreat began on 6th December: overwhelmingly superior numbers of Hanoverian redcoats were in pursuit…

Four months later and the scene switches to the Moray Coast where, on 15th April 1746, the Hanoverian army of 12,000 men were camped just south-west of Nairn. Their respected and feared commander was William Augustus, Duke of Cumberland, the second son of George II, and on that April day he happened to be celebrating his 25th birthday. Battle-hardened, he had seen action in Flanders and was now intent on eliminating the Jacobite threat once and for all by whatever means were necessary.

Meanwhile, just ten miles distant, Bonnie Prince Charlie and the Jacobite army had taken up positions east of Inverness where the Prince had requisitioned Culloden House as his headquarters. A planned surprise attack on the Duke's encampment under cover of darkness on the night of 15th April as the soldiers celebrated their commander's birthday had to be abandoned as poor reconnaissance left the Jacobites floundering in boggy terrain short of their objective. That experience, and the march back to Inverness, sapped physical strength and morale – factors of significance in the coming battle. The attacking force had been spotted, and as daylight came on the morning of 16th April the redcoats made ready to set off after the rebels.

·CULLODEN CASTLE·IN·1746·

Culloden Castle (or House) as it looked at the time of the "Forty-five". Owned at that time by Duncan Forbes, this was a building of considerable strength constructed around a square courtyard and robust enough to support a cannon on the roof.

Duncan Forbes, known as President Forbes, was Lord President of the Court of Session and Scotland's most senior judge. He was also an influential politician, strongly Protestant and in favour of the Union with England. A staunch supporter of the Hanoverian regime, his persuasive intervention had been pivotal in dissuading a number of clan chiefs from joining the uprising at an early stage, thereby depriving the Prince of 10,000 men – an act which viewed in the light of events could be said to have saved the throne. Despite this, the Prince on taking control of Culloden House, issued an order dated 28th February 1746 addressed to military personnel requiring them "to protect and defend the House of Culloden and furniture from any insults or violence that may be done by any person or persons."

Returning to the house at about 7 a.m. on the 16th April, he must have reflected that his prospects were diminishing. The planned surprise overnight attack at Nairn had come to nothing and his men were not only tired, but crucially short of food. The old saying that "an army marches on its stomach" was never truer, and his troops had not eaten for two days. He ordered them to forage for food over a wide area, including Inverness itself, which at that time could only just support its indigenous population. Prince Charlie had hardly taken to his bed when startling news was brought that the Hanoverians were closing in on Culloden Moor, two miles distant from Culloden House.

He left in haste to rally his commanders and all available troops to defend the road to Inverness, but with so many dispersed in the search for food, he may that day have fielded only half of his 5,000 men. From the Jacobite standpoint the wide, open, and sloping expanse of the moor was the worst possible terrain to engage the enemy. Cumberland's overwhelmingly numerically superior forces were massing on the bleak moor at 11 a.m., and from the outset the Jacobites were manoeuvred into a disadvantageous position: a north-easterly wind blew showers of rain and sleet into their faces, and they confronted the enemy on a slightly rising gradient. The Hanoverians were well-drilled and had undertaken some specific tactical training in the more effective use of the bayonet during previous weeks. Moreover, they had been well-provisioned by sea with food and supplies and, before a shot had been fired, the result of the coming conflict was never seriously in doubt.

The Battle of Culloden was not a battle between nations, or the English and the Scots. Culloden was a complex matter of dynasties, cultures, politics and religion: there were many more Scots in Cumberland's Hanoverian army than in the Prince's Highland force. For the Duke of Cumberland, this was not a "gentleman's war"; it was an uprising and as such the rebels were denied normal conventions and would be given no quarter.

Hostilities commenced at 1 p.m. and lasted about forty-five minutes of which, perhaps, only ten were in hand to hand combat. Prince Charlie's Highlanders possessed artillery, muskets and pistols but relied traditionally on one particular tactic – the Highland Charge. Accompanied by war cries, this was a wild, undisciplined dash designed to strike terror into the opposition. Equipped with broadsword and targe, deadly use was made of the dirk at close quarters. The Highlanders fought bravely, but such tactics were no match for the Hanoverian artillery which made full play of the open terrain to inflict appalling carnage.

In these few minutes any hope of a Stuart Restoration vanished. Prince Charles Edward Stuart – in tears, some say – reluctantly left the scene with a small body of trusted aides to flee down Strath Nairn via Tordarroch, Aberarder, Farraline and Gorthlick towards Fort Augustus and the west. His flight is almost as celebrated as the fight. With a price of £30,000 on his head, the fugitive survived to experience some extraordinary adventures before boarding a French ship in Loch nan Uamh which took him into exile on 20th September 1746.

Top: The Duke of Cumberland is said to have directed operations standing atop this boulder.
Above: King's Stables. Both *c.*1900.

In the aftermath of Culloden, Cumberland's forces are recorded as having seized "30 pieces of cannon, 2,320 firelocks, 190 broadswords, 37 barrels of powder and 22 carts of ammunition".

Owing to the fluidity of battle, estimates of casualties tend to vary, but commonly quoted figures, which may be conservative, are 1,200 Jacobites killed and 700 taken prisoner, against the loss of less than 100 Redcoats. The field was strewn with the dead, dying and injured, and in the blood-letting which followed a further 3,000 Highland men, women and children were slaughtered. As a Jacobite it was preferable to be one of the dead.

Graves of the Clans, Culloden   Valentines Series   20104

The atrocities that followed would for evermore confer on the Duke of Cumberland the sobriquet "Butcher". After his victory, he had taken temporary quarters at Culloden House, and legend has it that during a game of cards he scribbled on the back of the nine of diamonds the order to kill all the Highland wounded. They were everywhere, sheltering in barns and nearby houses; relentlessly hunted down, they were shot or bayoneted. Some lay on the bitter moor for two days – untreated by their own surgeons who had their instruments confiscated – before having their throats cut. Houses and barns found sheltering insurgents were put to the flames, some with the rebels securely locked inside to ensure their death. Back at Culloden House, seventeen Highland officers were imprisoned in the dungeon for three days before being taken out to be shot and bayoneted. Those that fled the field were pursued into Inverness. Homes were ransacked, the grammar school converted into the army's commissary and the town hall requisitioned as army headquarters. One church was destroyed and two others turned into prisons. In the parish churchyard a number of prisoners were summarily shot and their bodies thrown into a common grave. Such reprisals continued across the Highlands until the Prince was known to have escaped.

Duncan Forbes – descendant of President Forbes – was responsible for marking the clan graves (seen here 1894) and building the monumental cairn, twenty feet high by eighteen in diameter at which, on anniversaries, the Battle of Culloden is remembered.

Culloden has long been in the care of The National Trust for Scotland, and a new visitor centre costing £8 million was opened in December 2007 to replace facilities which had become inadequate. A long, sleek contemporary building incorporates state-of-the-art technology to provide sophisticated displays of original artefacts. The events of the "Forty-five" can be followed in a variety of presentations, but the one most likely to leave a lasting impression is the 'immersion theatre' – a small square cinema room where each wall offers a different camera perspective. Here visitors stand in this empty room to side either with the Jacobites or the Hanoverian army amidst the sights and sounds of conflict which eventually fade away leaving one to ponder the enormity of what has taken place. On the roof of the centre a terrace offers an uninterrupted view of the battlefield around which guided walks are available. This is a site which has great resonance in the history of our islands. Moreover, Culloden is a war grave and no one knows how many bodies lie here. Descendants of those who fought come to reflect, pay respects and mark the battle on anniversaries. This bleak moorland site has upwards of 250,000 visitors a year.

Mrs. Macdonald with Prince Charlie's C Battlefield Cottag Culloden Moor.

Often named Battlefield Cottage on postcards sold to the tourist trade before the First World War, and more correctly known as Leanach Cottage, an 1897 photograph in my collection is marked "Old Leanach House: where the Highlanders were massacred after the battle". However, information at the NTS Visitor Centre suggests that the stone cottage may have later replaced a turf hovel extant at the time of the battle, as a cannonball is recorded as having been recovered from a turf wall of that building in Victorian times. In the early 20th century, Mrs. Macdonald was a tenant and is seen here about 1900 holding 'Prince Charlie's Cup'. Was this the genuine article or a tourist gimmick, and has it survived? We may never know.

Culloden House today is the Georgian Palladian mansion of 1772 which replaced the castle, shown earlier. The new building is smaller than the original, and the front entrance formerly faced inwards across the courtyard. Duncan Forbes, a descendant of President Forbes, died in April 1897: a few months later in July that year the house contents were auctioned, and subsequently the house itself was sold. This view of Culloden House in 1888 was already 10 years old when the sender wrote this message, "This built by Duncan Forbes eminent patriot who 'provided' the battlefield. Prince Charlie stayed here night before the fight and left a lot of his gear. It's just outside Inverness and now for sale – wish I could afford it – superb Adam rooms within". The news that the historic contents, including many Jacobite treasures, of this famous house were to be sold and that A. Fraser and Co. of Union Street, Inverness (who else?) were preparing an inventory for an auction in July 1897 caused a sensation, generating interest from home and abroad. The auctioneers were only too aware that "the dispersal of furniture, relics and curios with hallowed recollections which surround an historical abode will naturally give rise to criticism of various kinds". How right they were, but Scotland did not have a National Trust at this time, and in England one had only recently been formed, acquiring its first property in 1896. An earlier *cause célèbre* related to Horace Walpole – politician, collector, writer and visionary: his collection of some 4,000 beautiful and precious objects was dispersed to the four winds in the sale of 1842 at Strawberry Hill. The Trust which administers the house is, even today, intent on tracing, borrowing or buying them back.

The hall, Culloden House, 1897.

Spectacular losses to our national history continue: many will recall the failure to retain houses and superb collections together at such properties as Mentmore Towers and Pitchford Hall despite enormous concern and public protest. Many iconic Jacobite related items were listed in the Culloden House sale catalogue of 1897, and I will refer to some of the most important shortly. Meanwhile, just to highlight one small example: the cannonball mentioned in the previous caption was sold to a Leeds doctor for £6. The history of that particular item is now lost. How much more interesting were it on display at Leanach Cottage today!

The special edition Purchasers' Catalogue issued after the sale includes purchasers' names and prices paid at the main three-day auction conducted at Culloden House in July 1897 when a total of 759 lots were sold. Lavishly illustrated with engravings and contemporary photographs, including interiors of the main rooms prior to sale, this rare publication gives a unique snapshot of the battlefield and this renowned house at the end of the Victorian era.

Dining Hall, Culloden House.

4162. 2.

Prince Charles' Bed, Culloden House.

The Dining Hall and the President's Room showing Prince Charlie's bed, 1897. The four poster mahogany bedstead was fourteen feet high with fine old chintz curtains and said to be in excellent order. Fully described on the following page as Lot No. 605, this historic item was purchased by J. Lawson Johnstone of London for £750. However, by 1930 it was back in Inverness and on display at Fraser's Museum of Antiquities in Union Street (the advertisement is shown on page 49). Thereafter the trail goes cold. Despite numerous enquiries, I have been unable to establish whether this highlight of the sale still exists and, if so, its whereabouts. Frasers discontinued their auction business several years ago, and a former employee said that much documentation had been lost in the 1950s fire which destroyed their depository in Falcon Square adjoining the station. Should any reader be able to shed further light on the famous bed I would be most interested to hear from them.

Limitation of space allows only the briefest of insights into this remarkable sale, and I have highlighted below just four particular lots which played a part in the events of April 1746.

A Case of Weapons, Relics &c. from Battlefield of Culloden

The high quality and vast range of house contents offered at the auction attracted buyers from near and far. Fine furniture, china, exquisite porcelain, glass, prints, engravings, oil paintings and rare Jacobite items mingled with small pieces and curios which had a special association with the house: locks and keys from the old castle, and a table, hall seat and letter weight made from an old pear tree in the orchard before the "Forty-five". There was a "quaint old billiard table – the first to be taken north", and a rare oil painting of the first St. Leger run in 1812, with a key listing owners and horses. Military items were, unsurprisingly heavily represented with many recovered from the battlefield: buttons, bullets, cannonballs, musket balls, dirks, swords, pistols, spurs, a Lochaber axe, claymores, bayonets, flintlock guns, gun barrels and a large horse pistol. Lot 718 was a carved Knob Kerrie "which had killed eight persons".

Lot 408. Prince Charles Edward's dining table. (Particulars abridged).

The old dining hall table was used by the Prince during his stay at Culloden Castle and, after the Battle of Culloden, by his cousin the Duke of Cumberland while he was in residence. Described as having a Shovel Board pattern, the table could be extended up to nearly twelve feet long, was massively carved and stood on six carved supports on a base. Sold to MacKintosh of MacKintosh of Moy Hall, £393 15s.

Lot 605. The Prince's bedstead.

"On reaching Culloden in his retreat northwards, Prince Charles Edward forcibly took possession of Culloden Castle, Lord President Forbes being obliged to flee for his life. The bed was used by him the three nights previous to the fateful battle. It is a massive mahogany tester bedstead, with beautifully carved foot pillars, and has the original hangings, valances etc."

Lot 647. Prince Charles Edward's walking stick.

"This was left leaning against the bed at Culloden Castle the night before the battle. As a handle it has two heads representing Folly and Wisdom. Presented to Queen Victoria by Colonel Warrand, and graciously accepted by Her Majesty".

Lot 670. Domino box, dominos and recorder.

"Left by William, Duke of Cumberland, at Culloden Castle after the 16th April 1746. Made of walrus ivory and bone. The royal insignia and monogram 'W' are cut from the solid ivory. Sold to MacKintosh of MacKintosh of Moy Hall, £55".

Duke of Cumberland's Domino Box

*   *   *   *

The sale of the century, maybe, but also a very significant loss to the heritage of the locality.

May Day at the Wishing Well, Culloden

Religion, mysticism, superstition and country lore are all associated with wells. Some are holy sites such as that shown earlier in Strath Glass, while others are wishing or clootie wells where coins are offered to accompany a wish, or a strip of rag or cloth is tied to a tree for a wish or a blessing. In Ireland such customs have a strong local tradition. Ascension Day in Derbyshire is still marked by well-dressing (the festal decoration of wells and springs). At Culloden on a May Day in the 1920s, evidently many turned out to make a wish, but recently at the visitor centre I was advised by a guide that "the event was not so well-attended these days". By the way he said it, I felt the custom was probably no longer observed. However, should this be the "well of the dead" that featured in the battle, then it has grim associations.

Leys Castle, Inverness

Leys Castle, 1918. The locally well-known Baillie family acquired the estate in 1712, and in 1833 Samuel Beazley (London theatre architect and playwright) designed this castellated and turreted mansion house for Colonel John Baillie M.P. After completion it was described as "a princely residence... all that wealth, skill and taste could render it". The house is the centrepiece of the superb mixed estate extending to over 3,000 acres just south of Inverness, and was placed on the market for sale at around £7 million in 2010.

A couple of miles west of the Leys Estate, overlooking the River Ness, is Ness Castle. Built as 'Darrochville' about 1820 for Lady Anne Maitland, wife of Robert Fraser of Torbreck, this has been described architecturally as a cottage-villa designed to an H-plan and having a distinctly smart interior. This image of 1913 shows part of the formal gardens and a rather marvellous Victorian greenhouse.

Aldourie House, Lochend, Loch Ness, c.1900. In 2002, the house (often incorrectly referred to as 'castle') was placed on the market together with 93 acres of the surrounding 3,000-acre estate, and offers of over £1.2 million were invited. The large Gothic baronial harled mansion of 1861 incorporated an earlier house which had itself been extended in 1839. Further modifications were made in 1902-3. The drawing-room incorporates a c.19th century marble chimney piece acquired at the Belladrum demolition sale mentioned previously. When Aldourie was marketed for sale, it had been in the ownership of the Cameron family and their ancestors for 300 years. As with so many properties, the huge 57-room house had simply become too large to manage and a financial liability. Nonetheless, the parting must have been painful.

Dores Bay

Dores Inn

General Wade is remembered less for his military exploits than for the road-building programme he undertook across the Highlands between 1725-33. His Inverness to Fort Augustus road has two branches at its northern end: one closely follows the line of river and loch via Dores, while the other is routed through Essich. Both converge at a point two miles south of Dores and Loch Ashie respectively. Dores, a small village attractively sited on a bay, an arm of Loch Ness, was laid out in 1820, and the inn – pictured here about 1907 – is believed to date from that period. Whether the two men feature in both photographs is uncertain, and although *something* has been caught, none of the group look particularly pleased!

Right: A timber team with their axes, circular saws and horses pose for this photograph against a stack of cut wood at Loch Ashie in 1910.

Centre: Strath Nairn, *c*.1905. After his defeat at Culloden in 1746, Prince Charlie and a few trusted aides fled this way towards Fort Augustus. The strath is characterised by open vistas, gentle hills, woods, neat farmsteads well-stocked with cattle and sheep – and many high quality sporting estates.

Below: When William and May Mackenzie acquired Farr House in 1892, it had already been enlarged by architect Alexander Ross in 1873/4; he aggrandised the earlier Georgian house of *c*.1780/90. In its heyday, Farr gave employment to some twenty-two staff, of whom ten worked the gardens and the 12,000-acre estate which extends 'over the hill' to Glenkyllachy Lodge on the River Findhorn. In the 1950s, the Duke of Gloucester regularly came each season for the stalking. However, by 1971 the 'Big House' had become quite uneconomic to run. Much too large and extensively affected by dry rot demolition became inevitable. This image about 1895 was taken by Inverness photographer David Whyte for the owners who used it as a Christmas card. (Photograph: Christopher J. Uncles Collection. ©: The Highland Photographic Archive, Highland Council).

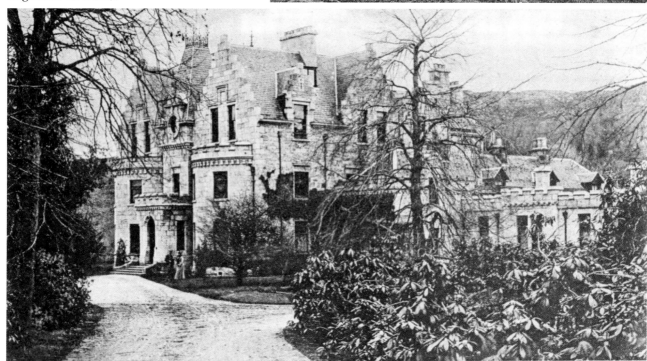

"Just received this card from Bella Cameron. That's old Cameron holding on to the fence with his grey beard flowing in the wind, it's the spit of him. I think that's Bella with the byke but it's hard to tell her; the others are strangers, but evidently in search of a stamp". Just part of a long message on this postcard mailed to Sydney, N.S.W. through Farr Post Office in 1906. This office has been closed for a number of years and postal business is currently transacted a mile away at the Inverarnie Stores where the original post office sign is carefully preserved.

Another 'Big House' in Strath Nairn, that at Brin, has seen much change over time. This image, prior to the First World War, provides a retrospective look at the house built by the Stuarts of Brin in 1862. Lying in the shelter of Brin Rock towering 600 feet behind the house to the west, the property was constructed of granite and roofed in slate, and overlooked the River Nairn to the east. Brin was designed around a courtyard and, as a Victorian estate house, had all the facilities one might expect ranging from billiard room and game larder to at least twelve bedrooms, some dedicated for staff use, on the first floor. Outbuildings included stables with a hayloft above, and an estate office to deal with the collection of rents and to supervise the game, fishing, forestry and stock-rearing activities.

Right: The road down Strath Nairn passes the entrance to Dunmaglass Lodge before joining General Wade's Military Road to Fort Augustus near Loch Mhór. There, an estate driveway fringes the northern end of the Loch for ½ mile to reach Farraline House, seen here about 1915.

Centre: A group of Farraline game-keepers and beaters assemble with their retrievers for a photograph before setting out for the moors and the seasonal ritual. At such times their role was to drive the grouse from the heather towards the gentry who would wait, fowling-pieces cocked, often concealed in waist-high circles of stone, timber and heather – known as the butts.

Below: The shooting party gathers along the roadside near Loch Mhór; the old milestone indicates the imminent division of routes, the mileages being Inverness 16, Craggie 15. Both images date from the early 1920s.

The 'quality' and the beaters take a break in the heather. Another view in this series (not shown) is annotated Ceoglas, Farraline, 17th August 1925. Under the Game Act of 1831, close seasons were established to protect game birds. To this day, game can be legally shot only during the following periods in Scotland: Red grouse and Ptarmigan (August 12th to December 10th); Snipe (August 12th to January 31st); Blackgame (August 20th to December 10th); Partridge (September 1st to February 1st); Pheasant (October 1st to February 1st) and Woodcock (September 1st to January 31st). Game cannot be shot on Sundays or on Christmas Day.

By permission of   "The Illustrated London News"

"Daybreak on the Twelfth"

This postcard of red grouse was mailed on the 'Glorious Twelfth' itself in 1902 and shows birds, rather pointedly, at 'daybreak'. Grouse moors require intensive management, and owing to natural predators, tick infestation or poor weather (especially during the breeding season), yields can vary enormously from year to year. Each August witnesses an unseemly rush to deliver game to top restaurants throughout the country in the shortest possible time after the 'Twelfth' so that menus can feature 'new season's grouse' at premium prices. Resist the temptation and your dining experience will be much improved; grouse, as with all game, needs to be hung for a few days which enhances the flavour immeasurably.

Inverfarigaig has breathtaking views across the expanse of Loch Ness. Somewhat off the beaten tourist track, this hidden gem is often missed. Minor roads, including that through the pass, small ravines, rushing streams over peat-stained pools and lichen-covered boulders are all contained within a well-wooded landscape which combine to evoke an almost secret and ethereal Shangri-la. The woods are home to badgers, deer and pine marten.

Inverfarigaig Pier, 1891. In those days tourist steamers made a call en route to the famous Falls of Foyers, two miles distant – that was before they were harnessed for industrial purposes in 1896. Later, Inverfarigaig had a link with Achnahannet on the opposite shore of the loch, but that sailboat ferry ceased operations in the 1920s.

On the Dores-Foyers road alongside Loch Ness, c.1955; another stretch engineered by the General and his redcoats.

Opposite Foyers Post Office a commemorative stone is inscribed 'Falls of Foyers 1896-1996. In recognition of the pioneers of aluminium production at Foyers. British Alcan Aluminium'.

Aluminium is derived from the ore bauxite, first discovered in 1821, and is produced in a two-stage process. Firstly the bauxite is converted, by chemical means, to aluminium oxide (alumina) which is then reduced by electrolysis to produce commercially-pure aluminium. Large amounts of electricity are required and water power is the favoured and relatively economical driving force. That fact was influential in bringing the great Victorian innovator, Lord Kelvin, and the North British Aluminium Company to Foyers in 1894 to build Britain's first industrial hydro-electric power station and aluminium smelter.

The 7250-acre Lower Foyers Estate was acquired along with water rights covering a catchment area in Stratherrick where Lochs Garth and Farraline were merged to become Loch Mhór. The River Foyers and its upper and lower waterfalls, which had a combined drop of 120 feet and were formerly regarded as the most magnificent in Britain, were harnessed to the lasting detriment of their scenic beauty. There was no local labour force of any size, and everything required to build and operate the plant, together with the materials needed for a new village which eventually housed 600 people, was brought in by sea to the pierhead on Loch Ness. The return cargoes of processed ingots and rolling slabs were similarly conveyed to a Staffordshire mill.

Almost immediately, Foyers was producing 200 tons of aluminium – some 10% of the world demand at that time when the metal had semi-precious status. This highly imaginative landmark in Highland development must have shaken this previously quiet backwater – used only to tourists intent on viewing the famous falls – to its foundations. By the 1960s the metal had become increasingly common worldwide and in everyday use, and the factory closed.

Glendoe Lodge

Valentines Series   43160

GLENDOE LODGE, FORT AUGUSTUS

A.1344.   FORT AUGUSTUS FROM GLEN DOE.

The recently commissioned Glendoe Power Station is the largest hydro-station project built in Britain for 50 years and, as at Foyers a century earlier, harnesses water collected in the hills above Loch Ness for power generation. A 905-metre low-level dam across the River Tarff has created a body of water which can be released through tunnels to an underground power station housing the turbine set 608 metres below the reservoir. This is the highest 'drop' of any hydro-station in the United Kingdom; subsequently, the waters are returned to Loch Ness. The turbine can be activated to meet increased demand as required and can reach full capacity in just 30 seconds, generating enough power for a city the size of Glasgow.

Glendoe Lodge is seen here about 1904, together with its position on the hillside above Loch Ness and Fort Augustus. In that image, c.1938, note the monastery (centre), formerly a military fort which is featured in the ensuing section. Meanwhile, we move a few miles north-west of Fort Augustus to Glen Moriston.

GLEN MORISTON TO LOCH LINNHE.

How many motorists hurrying westwards by the long road between Invermoriston and Shiel Bridge notice a small cairn by the roadside near Ceannacroc Lodge in Glen Moriston? Known as Roderick Mackenzie's Cairn, an extraordinary event in July 1746 is commemorated at this spot. After the events of Culloden, 'Butcher' Cumberland marched his troops south to Fort Augustus, taking up residence at the fort and masterminding a reign of terror in the surrounding glens in an effort to capture the fugitive Prince Charlie, on whose head lay a ransom of £30,000. In the ensuing weeks of repression, redcoat patrols and raiding parties ravaged the countryside, indiscriminately killing civilians and driving others from their hovels, byres and black houses which were set alight leaving them homeless. No quarter was given by the Hanoverian forces as whole settlements in the glens were put to the flames. In Glen Moriston, Mackenzie was apprehended by a party of redcoats. The cairn declares he was a Jacobite officer, while other sources say he was a pedlar, but on one point all accounts agree: he bore a striking likeness to Prince Charlie. As he lay dying from his wounds he declared, "You have killed your Prince". Maybe with the £30,000 reward in mind, the soldiers cut off his head and returned triumphantly with it to the Duke of Cumberland at Fort Augustus. On receiving further positive identification from Jacobite prisoners held at the fort, Cumberland hastened south to London with the head only to learn there that he had been hoodwinked. The consequent delay, deception and distraction is said to have enabled Prince Charlie to make good his escape. However, on one aspect there is no doubt: the selfless action of Mackenzie has elevated his name to legendary status in the history of the "Forty-five".

Footnote: I subsequently came across this extract written by folklorist Calum Iain Maclean (1915-60) in his book *The Highlands*: "Mackenzie's headless body was buried near the roadway beside a little stream that to this day bears the name of Caochan à Cheannaich – 'the Merchant's Stream'". This reinforces my belief that the wording on the cairn is incorrect, and that Mackenzie was indeed a travelling merchant (pedlar).

Edwardian stalking party in Glen Moriston, 1906. The extensive hill country either side of the glen provides classic terrain for stalking and fishing, activities which still continue to sustain the many sporting lodges throughout the glen.

Wild Cat   Captured at Glen Moriston

Scottish Wildcat (*Felis silvestris grampia*) captured in Glen Moriston, *c.*1905. The Wildcat population was isolated in Britain at the end of the last Ice Age, but is thought to have lived in Europe for more than ten million years. Persecuted to extinction in England and Wales by the 1860s, the pure breed, as distinct from wild (feral) cats, clings on precariously in pockets of the Highlands, the Grampians, Black Isle, Aberdeenshire and Ardnamurchan. Estimates are uncertain and range from just 400 to several thousand. Some specimens can measure up to four feet from nose to tail. Other distinguishing features are the fierce, untameable spirit, muscular appearance and the bushy tail with three to five black rings ending in a blunt tip which is always black.

Torgyle Bridge, 1934. The three-arched bridge, built in 1825-6 to replace an earlier structure swept away by floods seven years previously, is particularly fine: rounded tower supports decorated with cross-slits rise above the cut-waters to ornate battlemented parapets. This strategically important crossing of the River Moriston was used by cattle drovers until late Victorian times. Driving their beasts over the hills from Strath Glass and Guisachan, they joined the old military road down to Fort Augustus before proceeding over the Corrieyairack Pass and onwards to the trysts at Crieff and Falkirk. For today's travellers the bridge is a link in the road through Glen Moriston – a scenic route, via dramatic Glen Shiel, to Wester Ross and Skye.

Torgyle Lodge, built about 1903 and once part of the Grant Estates, lies on what was formerly the main road through Glen Moriston to Skye. Today the porch is a little different and there is a more formal frontage to the old road.

During the summer of 1919 this group of stylish people came to Torgyle to engage in their passion for fishing. They came with their dogs and fine cars to try their luck on hill loch and river, leaving a record of their excursions in an album of over 100 photographs. Their vehicles often filled the narrow width of the primitive roads, and while a number of locations are not identified, others have changed owing to the passage of time. In particular, the Garry-Moriston Hydro-Electric Scheme, completed in the 1950s, resulted in dramatic changes as lochs were dammed and river flows altered. The level of Loch Cluanie was raised by over 29 metres while on the River Moriston, the Bobbin Pool which they fished, was probably lost by the construction of the underground power station at Dundreggan.

In the photographic album the lochs at Cluanie, Liath, Lundie and Stac feature prominently. Scenes on riverbank or lochside are accompanied with rods afloat on dinghies. Some remote lochs are reached using creel-carrying ponies, while another photograph shows a pony pulling a small trailer with dinghy atop in order to fish a location in particularly difficult terrain. Picnics are shown, including some at a little 'tower house' building at Loch Stac, said by locals to have been built by the noted wildlife artist, the late H. Frank Wallace, for his honeymoon. At the end of each day, Torgyle Lodge beckoned. Here they would proudly display and photograph the day's catch on the gable wall (*above*), or stage a montage in the front porch (*below*). This photograph is annotated "Loch Cluanie trout, weight 3 lbs. 4 ozs., July 1919. Caught on a grouse and purple". While the activities of this group are so well recorded, unfortunately thus far the identities of the individuals themselves remain elusive.

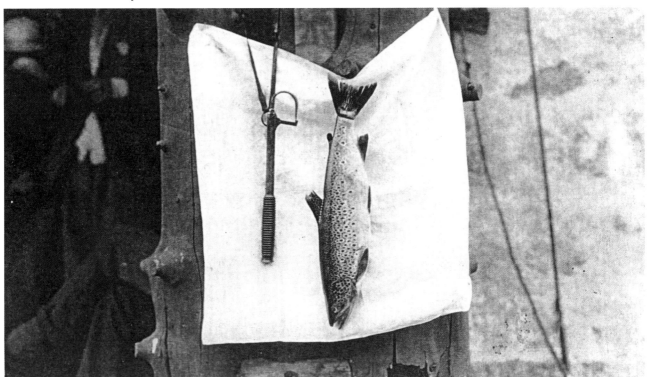

OLD AND NEW BRIDGES, ALLTSAIGH LOCH NESS

Roads around Invermoriston.

Top: Old and new bridges at Alltsaigh after the lochside road improvements of 1925-33. In the distance, the Half Way House was once a tea room/small hotel before becoming a SYHA youth hostel in June 1943.

Centre: The 'new road' by Loch Ness awaits resurfacing, 1932.

Below: Invermoriston, *c*.1954. A tantalising choice of route for the tourist: bear left for Fort William by the Great Glen, or straight ahead for Glen Moriston and Skye. For a decision of this magnitude, adjournment to the hotel might be advisable!

AT INVERMORISTON, INVERNESS-SHIRE.

Pictured in the 1930s, the strategically placed Glenmoriston Arms Hotel lies alongside historic routes which converge here. The present building, believed to date from the 19th century, is unlikely to have been the first on this site. Displayed in the bar is an interesting collection of old local photographs and postcards, trade invoices and business tariffs, together with a map showing the extent of the former Glen Moriston Estate.

Opposite the hotel, the strangely named hill of Sròn na Muic ("Pig's snout") rises behind the general store. Such businesses were the mainstay of small communities, including the scattering of sporting lodges which required provisioning especially when the gentry came north for the shooting season. At a time when there was no mass communication, which we take for granted today, there was also a social dimension: news could be passed on and messages left. This pre-First World War image indicates that facilities are available for the motorist, and that a boot and shoe maker also occupied the premises. Note the barefooted youngsters; it would not have been unusual to be without shoes between May and September. Nearby, the waters of an ancient roadside well believed to have existed since Pictish times, are said to have been blessed and made pure by St. Columba in A.D. 565.

Invermoriston House, seen here about 1909 and superbly sited overlooking Loch Ness, was the "Big House" of the extensive lands once owned by successive Grants of Glenmoriston. However, about 1930, it was gutted by fire after a dreadful accident caused, the story goes, when a maid left a lit candle near some curtains which caught alight. This was the third house to be built here; the previous two were also consumed by flames being deliberately destroyed during the Jacobite risings of 1715 and 1745. In 1988 the estate was broken up and sold, including a smaller, modern Invermoriston House.

The River Moriston ("river of waterfalls") enters Loch Ness at Invermoriston. Left of the modern bridge, constructed in 1933 to meet increased demands of vehicular traffic, stands Thomas Telford's bridge commenced in 1805. Taking eight years to complete, the inordinate delay was blamed on "idle workers" and "languid and inattentive contractors". As a result, the guarantor of the scheme, Sir John Campbell of Ardnamurchan, sustained a loss of £200.

Invermoriston Pier, 1904. The Loch Ness steamer arriving at the pierhead was an important link landing all manner of goods, and no doubt a few tourists, at a time when roads were primitive. A horse and cart stands ready to leave for the village. Today the site is privately owned and little remains of the old pier.

Railway Pier and Loch Ness, Fort Augustus

The small village of Fort Augustus at the southern end of Loch Ness – a handful of houses and a Benedictine Monastery – quite extraordinarily found itself with two railway stations in the early years of the 20th century. Promoted by the Invergarry and Fort Augustus Railway, the 24-mile line from Spean Bridge was ill-conceived from the outset, over-engineered at lavish cost and failed to meet the quite unrealistic expectations of its shareholders. First sods were cut in 1897 and the railway opened in July 1903. However, a profit was never generated, and the Pier Station seen here in 1903, closed just three years later in 1906.

FORT AUGUSTUS.

Fort Augustus, c.1937 showing the road from Invermoriston (bottom right). The village is sliced in two by Thomas Telford's Caledonian Canal, the banks of which were lined originally by shops and businesses to attract tourists from passing steamers. The bridge of 1934 across the River Oich (foreground) replaced a much earlier structure closer to Loch Ness for which restoration funds are currently being sought.

Fort Augustus. The Locks.

From the locks about 1915 showing the Benedictine Monastery (centre), Loch Ness and the small 'pepper-pot' lighthouse (left). Men either side of the tow path are turning the capstans to open and close the gates. Quite demanding physically, each operation required seven revolutions. These days, the push of a button and the combination of electricity and hydraulic power works the miracle.

Lovat Arms Hotel, Fort Augustus

The Lovat Arms and Station Hotel was built by the ill-fated Invergarry and Fort Augustus Railway in 1903 on the site of the first military barracks erected here following the rising of 1715. The twin barrack buildings of 1718-19 were constructed by Government forces under the direction of General George Wade to accommodate about 100 soldiers; a section of the western rampart wall survives as the earliest locally listed monument (author's photograph). In those days the village took its name of Kilcumein from Cille-chumein, the church or cell of Cumein, an Abbott of Iona. About 1729 Wade changed the Gaelic name to Fort Augustus in honour of the youthful Prince William Augustus, later the notorious Duke of Cumberland.

*   *   *   *

"If you'd seen the road before it was made, you'd bless the name of General Wade" was the old couplet, but it should be said that the General's widespread engineering activities across the Highlands between the years 1725-1733 were part of a pacification scheme following the Jacobite Rising of 1715 which was regarded by the Highland chiefs and their clansmen with the utmost suspicion and hostility. Situated mid-way on the General's military road between Inverness and Fort William, Fort Augustus became of considerable strategic importance which was further enhanced by the construction of a linking road built by some 500 redcoats through wild country over the Corrieyairack Pass. This facilitated the movement and passage of troops and supplies with the Ruthven Barracks, near Kingussie. The pass rose steeply to over 2,500 feet above sea level, and the crowning achievement of Wade's route over the pass was the construction of seventeen (later reduced to thirteen) zigzags or traverses, each measuring 70-80 yards in length. Various travellers have left dramatic accounts of their journeys, especially in winter, and the horse, cattle and sheep drovers of old used this "green road" until the closing years of Queen Victoria's reign to bring their beasts through the hills to the trysts of Crieff and Falkirk.

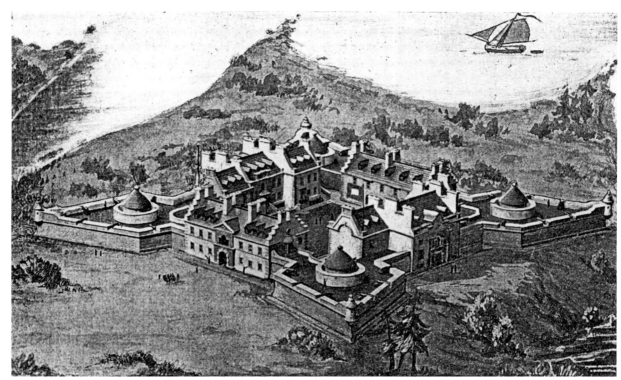

Significant events in the history of the new fort (*above*) in brief:

1725   King George I authorises the building of a more secure fortification beside Loch Ness.
1729   General Wade sets about land acquisition and construction begins.
1742   Building completed – "of very considerable strength and having splendid masonry".
1746   March: Jacobite forces land a lucky shot on powder-magazine; garrison surrenders. Two months later, Cumberland arrives to find fort badly damaged.
         September: 2,000 troops stationed locally; restoration of fort underway.
1773   Dr. Samuel Johnson and James Boswell stop here on their famous tour to be agreeably entertained by Lieutenant-Governor Trapaud and his family before continuing onwards over the military road to Glen Moriston and Skye. Alexander Trapaud was Lieutenant-Governor here for 44 years (1752-96).
1803   Thomas Telford commences work on the Caledonian Canal.
1818   Last regular soldiers leave the fort; armaments removed.

FORT AUGUSTUS ABBEY. The Monastery

The Abbey School, Fort-Augustus.   "The Abbey Press," Fort-Augustus.

In 1876 Lord Lovat purchased the 20-acre fort and farm site from the government and created a lease to Benedictine monks for a monastery to be established in accordance with the strict rule of St. Benedict. Building commenced and continued for the next 100 years as selected portions of the old fort were absorbed into various monastic buildings – monastery, college, hospice, school, library and scriptorium. In 1889 the monks installed the first hydro-electric scheme in Scotland, with surplus capacity lighting Fort Augustus streets until 1951. The church was consecrated in 1890. The standard of work externally and internally was of the highest order, and architects of national repute were engaged. Well before the First World War over £150,000 had been expended. *Above*: the monastery from the gardens, and the Abbey School, *c*.1919 – a postcard printed by The Abbey Press.

Pax in virtute
Peace with Righteousness
(the Abbey motto.)

"The Hospice is on the college side. Fort Augustus has a village of 400 people and there is also an inn in the village. The abbey has no vehicles so that the auto of a European model is that of a visitor". (Undated message).

An original wall of the military fort. In late Victorian times it was necessary to pierce a doorway through one of the bastions: the mason took three whole days to breach the wall!

Old Bastion Wall, Fort Augustus

THE MUSEUM, FORT AUGUSTUS ABBEY

The Abbey Museum, *c.*1915. The library had capacity for 30,000 books.

Footnote: This colossal Grade A listed building was horrendously demanding to maintain. As a result, the Abbey School closed in 1993, and the dwindling community of monks departed five years later. After a period of uncertainty and understandable local concern, the Highland Club acquired the property for conversion into 80 luxury apartments and twelve cottages, the final phase being due for completion in 2011.

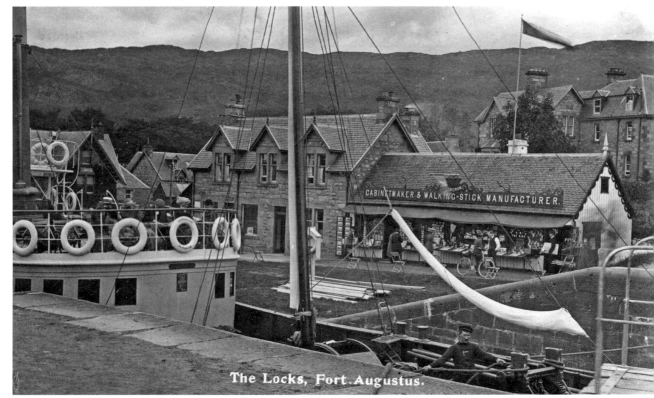

The Locks, Fort Augustus.

Two well-known local institutions captured at Thomas Telford's engineering masterpiece at Fort Augustus – the staircase of five locks built 1817 – 21. The first is the most famous of all vessels which sailed the Caledonian Canal, namely P.S. *Gondolier*; the Inverness-Banavie route was the regular scene of her operations between 1866 – 1939. The other is Cameron's canalside emporium ("Patronised by H.M. The King") which sold Highland books, golf clubs, views, postcards, walking sticks and much else to attract tourists killing time as steamers negotiated the locks.

In the Locks, Fort Augustus.

An 'each-way' perspective in the locks at Fort Augustus about 1900. The five lock flight is one of three 'staircases' along the Caledonian Canal and lowers vessels 40 feet to Loch Ness. The time-consuming manual operation of the capstans gave ample opportunity for passengers to stretch their legs ashore, visit canalside shops and tea rooms or walk across to the monastery. In Victorian times a real surprise awaited them: "There was always the chance of an encounter with Roualeyn George Gordon Cumming, an aristocratic eccentric, whose contribution to the gaiety of Highland life has never been fully recognised. Followed by his manservant and a long-bearded goat, he would invite passengers to inspect his famous museum collection, at a 'bob a nob', while their boat negotiated the canal locks. Gordon Cumming was an attraction as unusual as his collection of skins and heads. He sported a kilt and plaid of Gordon tartan with top boots, frilled shirt and masses of jewels, a brass helmet on his head and silver fish-hooks in his ears. An enthusiastic nudist, he discarded his kilt on hot days". (*The Highlands and Islands of Scotland* by Allan Campbell McLean, 1976).

Invergarry Castle stands perched high above the waters of Loch Oich on Creag an Fhithich (the "Raven's Rock"). This surviving stronghold of the MacDonells of Glengarry was built in the early 17th century either for Donald MacDonnell of Glengarry or his heir, but is certainly not the first fortification on this site. Connected with one of these buildings is a marvellous legend: The stones were obtained from Ben Tee, five miles away. A line of men stretched from there to the site, and the stones were passed from man to man until they reached the builders! In 1645 General Monk reported that his troops had burned "Glengaries new house", but by 1691 repairs had resulted in a stronghold which could not be taken without "great cannon". In the "Forty-five" Prince Charlie briefly sheltered here on two occasions; as a result the Duke of Cumberland's forces took revenge. The castle was blown up and burned in the sight of its inhabitants who were 'shepherded' to the hillside so that they should miss no pang of defeat. Invergarry Castle was abandoned thereafter, remaining a gaunt, picturesque ruin.

The ruins of the castle lie within the wooded policies of Invergarry House, now a country house hotel known as the Glengarry Castle Hotel. Architect David Bryce chose an attractive lochside position for his Scottish baronial mansion built in 1869, as confirmed by a date-stone above the entrance porch. As befitting the period, rooms are well proportioned, while somewhat unusually on several external walls are stone tablets bearing phrases such as "With thy blessing let the house of thy servant be blessed for ever" and "A merciful man will be merciful to his beast". A stable block was added 1875-6. A past owner was Edward Ellice, Liberal M.P. for the St. Andrews burghs from 1837 to 1880, who did much for the estate.

THE WELL OF THE SEVEN HEADS, LOCH OICH. A.3672.

AS a memorial of the ample and summary vengeance which in the swift course of Feudal Justice inflicted by the orders of the Lord McDonell and Aross overtook the perpetrators of the foul murder of the Keppoch family, a branch of the powerful and illustrious clan of which his lordship was the chief. This monument is erected by Colonel McDonell of Glengarry XVII. Mac-Mhic Alaister, his successor and representative, in the year of our Lord 1812.

The heads of the seven murderers were presented at the feet of the noble chief in Glengarry Castle after having been washed in the spring, and ever since that event which took place early in the sixteenth century it has been known by the name of "Tobar nan Ceann" or the Well of the Seven Heads.

R.M.S. Gondolier passing R.M.S. Gairlochy LochOich.
Jackson's Series, Kinlochleven.

Paddy at Laggan Locks.

Top: Postscript – a Fort William antiquary is known to have found and excavated the murderers' burial mound at Inverlair; all seven skeletons were headless which gives some credence to this grisly event.

Left: P. S. *Gairlochy* was brought on to the canal to double with *Gondolier* from 1895. However, on Christmas Eve 1919 she was gutted by fire at Fort Augustus where her hull can still be seen off Inveroich Pier at times of low water.

Right: Flamboyantly dressed, Paddy was a lockside entertainer at Laggan, *c*.1900 where such people had a captive audience as steamers negotiated the locks, but little seems known about him.

Ben Nevis from the Ranch.

The Autumn Round-up.

THE GREAT GLEN CATTLE RANCH.

One of the Shelters.

Achandaul Farm.

Land, its uses, management and ownership have all long been issues engendering vigourous debate in the Highlands. Periodically an individual emerges possessing particular knowledge, dedication and conviction coupled with the ability to demonstrate an innovative way of doing things. One such person was the ecologist Dr. (later Sir) Frank Fraser Darling, who in 1938 transformed the barren island of Tanera More in Wester Ross into a productive farm – an achievement which attracted national interest. Another such man with exceptional qualities was the late J. W. Hobbs who came to Lochaber in 1944; his vision embraced the intensification of cattle rearing by better land use. After implementing a spectacular programme of land improvement and reclamation on the Inverlochy Estate, between Fort William and Spean Bridge, he very successfully established the Great Glen Cattle Ranch for these purposes. This land-holding was enlarged further when he bought out and amalgamated some underused crofts at Brackletter. Sheep were excluded from the 10,000-acre estate, and breeding cows kept in top condition by feeding silage made from oats, peas, beans and tares grown on reclaimed land. Mr. Hobbs also owned the Ben Nevis Distillery, and cattle feed was supplemented by distillery draff which proved a useful by-product contributing to lower costs. The proprietor's pioneering vision and enthusiasm created what is generally regarded as a landmark development in the Great Glen, giving a boost to employment and the local economy.

High Bridge, Speanbridge

Built by General Wade in 1736 to move troops and supplies across the dramatic Spean Gorge, High Bridge must have been quite imposing standing as it did 100 feet above the swiftly flowing waters of the river. Although the bridge, pictured in 1894, subsequently collapsed, the site has found a niche in history as the place where the opening shots of the "Forty-five" were fired. On 16th August 1745 Donald MacDonell of Tirnadrish with eleven men and a piper made use of the surrounding woods to disguise the smallness of their numbers, and successfully waylaid a detachment of 85 government troops sent from Fort Augustus to reinforce the garrison at Fort William. Four redcoats were killed and several wounded; their commanding officer, Captain Scott, was wounded and taken prisoner. The Highlanders suffered no losses.

Fort William   *Achnacarry Castle*

That portion of Lochaber lying to the east of the Loch and River Lochy is the area earliest identified with Clan Cameron. The ancient residence of Lochiel was Tor Castle, erected by Ewen Cameron (XIII) of Lochiel in the early 16th century, and it remained the seat of the family until Sir Ewen (XVII) of Lochiel (1629-1719) built a mansion for himself at Achnacarry about 1650. Achnacarry, the modern seat of Cameron of Lochiel, is situated in a wooded landscape between Lochs Lochy and Arkaig at the foot of Glen Caig, once part of the famous drovers' route from Skye and Glen Garry. The locality has strong associations with the "Forty-five"; Prince Charles Edward Stuart and his followers came this way on their westward flight, taking refuge in bothies and caves around the Mile Dorcha ("Dark Mile"), so-called because thick foliage from trees overshadowed the rough track at that time. Support for the Prince cost Lochiel dearly; temporary exile and the burning of Achnacarry followed as the countryside was wasted after Culloden. Following the eventual restoration of the forfeited estate, the house (pictured here) was rebuilt between 1802 and 1837. During the Second World War the house became a centre for Commandos undergoing training over large areas of Lochaber. While Achnacarry House is not open to the public, the Clan Cameron Museum is a 'must' for those interested in clan and regimental history as well as Jacobite and Commando artefacts.

At Gairlochy, three miles south of Achnacarry, a lock-keeper's house overlooks the canal. Thomas Telford often stayed here, especially during the construction phase; the first floor room with bow-windows (known as Telford's Room) provided an excellent vantage point in both directions from which he could observe and monitor progress as his Caledonian Canal took shape. (Author's photograph).

Reached by a short diversion from the minor road between Gairlochy and Banavie, Telford's Tunnels carry the Caledonian Canal above the Sheangain Burn. One arch of the aqueduct, more suited to the days of horse and wagon, does permit small vehicles a crossing with care, as the interior is somewhat dim and dank. Nearby are the scant but picturesque remains of Tor Castle which are traditionally believed to have been the house of Banquo, 10th century Thane of Lochaber, immortalised in Shakespeare's *Macbeth*. Clan Mackintosh held lands here prior to their acquisition by the Camerons.

A shooting lodge built in Victorian times subsequently became the Torcastle Hotel, but a dreadful fire sealed its fate abruptly in the summer of 1950. Jim Lee of Banavie, whose aunt and uncle owned the hotel at the time, recounted the circumstances. The property, then lit by gas, was in the process of being wired for mains electricity when a fault developed starting a serious fire which soon passed out of control. The fire brigade was summoned, but the tender was too large to negotiate the tunnel, forcing the crew to return to Banavie in an effort to access the canal bank and tackle the blaze from there. By that time the hotel was quite beyond saving, and the speed of the conflagration resulted in few contents surviving. Guests already booked, and new arrivals, had to be hastily re-accommodated locally. The ruins were eventually demolished and the stonework removed to be used as infilling for the West End Car Park in Fort William.

Lochiel Arms Hotel, Banavie, *c.*1873. The view of Ben Nevis, Britain's highest mountain at 4,406 feet, loomed large and majestic from this famous hotel's windows, while a few steps from the front door lay the Caledonian Canal (centre) with Neptune's Staircase and the steamer landing-stage. Little wonder that the hotel was always busy with 'one-nighters' sailing up from Oban in the afternoon, dining and sleeping, before walking across to the canal to join the Inverness steamer after breakfast the following morning. They were travelling part of 'The Royal Route', so-called because Queen Victoria had come this way in 1873; she had enthused about the wonders of Telford's engineering, but had found the journey itself "very tedious". Built in 1848 the 'Lochiel' enjoyed an excellent reputation and, by 1890, over 100 guests could be accommodated. Later photographs show further enlargement and a change of name to the Banavie Hotel. But, disaster struck comprehensively in 1924 when the hotel was gutted by fire (below); the stark ruins stood until demolition about 1935. There is a belief locally that a spark from an open fire in a bedroom may have caused the blaze.

A residential development took place on part of the former vegetable garden *c.*1936/7, the stables were demolished and four houses built on that site. The former laundry, bakery and staff quarters became a hostel. (Lower photograph reproduced here by kind permission of the West Highland Museum, Fort William.)

The Pier, Banavie

Those who have followed the journey thus far will be familiar with the *Gondolier* – seen at Banavie landing-stage (above) in 1924, the westerly extremity of her operations. Here, opposite the Lochiel Arms Hotel, passengers boarded and disembarked alongside a short spur (left) which connected with the West Highland Railway. While there must have been a sense of expectation and anticipation in the air for those about to leave, arrivals from Muirtown had been water-borne for eight hours along 'the grand corridor of Scotland' and would have much to talk about over dinner in Fort William. *Below*: Just beyond the stage is Neptune's Staircase, another of Telford's engineering masterpieces. On this massive eight-lock flight, 900 men laboured for four years between 1807-11. Vessels entering the staircase are lowered by eight feet through each lock, a total of 64 feet before reaching Corpach Basin. For Telford's navvies, this too was slow work as the basin had to be cut from solid rock using only hand tools. At Corpach, the western end of the 60-mile waterway through the Great Glen, the open waters of Loch Linnhe are entered, just three miles north-west of Fort William.

Neptune's Staircase, Banavie

Valentines Series